Praise for Love 'Em or Lose 'Em

"Not only will this book help you attract and retain the best and most motivated employees, it will also help you create and lead engaged employees. This book is a must-read for aspiring leaders and those looking for better results in the workplace."

—C. Michael Abrashoff, author of *It's Your Ship* and *Get Your Ship Together*

"With knowing wit and practical intelligence Beverly Kaye and Sharon Jordan-Evans present us with elegant solutions and engaging examples of how to deal with the most vexing problem organizations now confront—engaging and retaining the very best talent."

—Jim Kouzes, co-author of *The Leadership Challenge*

"Kaye and Jordan-Evans provide some of the best thinking I've seen on the subject of retention and engagement."

—Steve Bauman, Vice President of Workforce Development, Marriott International

---

"Terrifically practical tips, advice, admonition and just plain fun ideas to ensure that your best and brightest don't take a hike."

—Skip Corsini, *Training Magazine*

"Today, more than ever, leaders must be able to develop and retain talent for their own organizations. Love 'Em or Lose 'Em: Getting Good People to Stay *is packed with practical advice on how this challenging and critical task can be accomplished."*

—John R. Alexander President, Center for Creative Leadership

"In the war for talent, Synopsis has chosen Love 'Em or Lose 'Em *as our prime field manual. As practical as it is insightful and thorough, this book has given our managers the principles and practices they need to retain our best and brightest people."*

—Aart J. de Geus, Chairman and CEO, Synopsis, Inc.

"Your no-nonsense approach to retention was a BIG hit with a very tough audience. Since our convention there are signs of 'Love 'Em' everywhere, positively impacting our managers' approach to their people."

—Mari Anne Snow, Director of Training, Uno Restaurant Corporation.

"This gives our managers practical tools to use the very next day, along with inspiration to meet their goals."

—June Chrisman, Director, Human Resources, Providence Health System Oregon

---

"Aimed squarely at managers who ordinarily reject, refute, and 'yeah-but' all the trite touchy-feely, overly saccharine, and unrealistically techniquey advice about motivating people."

—Don Blohowiak, "Lead Well® Institute"

"Motivating top talent is perhaps the most critical task a manager performs. The authors offer creative tips for doing that—and then some."

—Cord Cooper, national newspaper columnist

"A great business book for this millennium. Retain it and your business will prosper."

—Bob Rosner, author of the syndicated column "Working Wounded" and *The Boss's Survival Guide*

"Down-to-earth and practical, it gives managers, supervisors, and leaders things that they can do tomorrow—no, today—to stop the brain-drain. You'd better read it before your best folks set sail for elsewhere."

—Bill Bridges, author of *Transitions, Job Shift, and You, Inc.*

"Love 'Em or Lose 'Em offers busy managers a fresh viewpoint that clearly links business success to retention of talent."

—Richard J. Leider, Founder, the Inventure Group, co-author of *Claiming Your Place at the Fire: Living the Second Half of Your Life on Purpose*

"Love 'Em or Lose 'Em has sharpened our leaders' awareness of the costs of losing talent and the benefits associated with retention-focused management strategies. . . . We saw an immediate increase in the degree of active responsibility taken by many of our managers to retain our key employees."

—John Madigan, Vice President, Corporate Staffing, The Hartford Insurance Group

LOVE 'EM
— OR —
LOSE 'EM

Other books by Beverly Kaye and Sharon Jordan-Evans

Love It, Don't Leave It: 26 Ways to Get What You Want at Work

Up Is Not the Only Way

Learning Journeys

LOVE 'EM

— OR —

LOSE 'EM

GETTING GOOD PEOPLE TO STAY

BEVERLY KAYE AND SHARON JORDAN–EVANS

BERRETT-KOEHLER PUBLISHERS, INC.
San Francisco

Berrett-Koehler Publishers, Inc.
235 Montgomery St., Suite 650
San Francisco, CA 94104-2916
Tel: (415) 288-0260   Fax: (415) 362-2512   www.bkconnection.com

ORDERING INFORMATION

Quantity sales. Special discounts are available on quantity purchases by corporations, associations, and others. For details, contact the "Special Sales Department" at the Berrett-Koehler address above.

Individual sales. Berrett-Koehler publications are available through most bookstores. They can also be ordered direct from Berrett-Koehler: Tel: (800) 929-2929; Fax: (802) 864-7626; www.bkconnection.com

Orders for college textbook/course adoption use. Please contact Berrett-Koehler: Tel: (800) 929-2929; Fax: (802) 864-7626.

Orders by U.S. trade bookstores and wholesalers. Please contact Publishers Group West, 1700 Fourth Street, Berkeley, CA 94710. Tel: (510) 528-1444; Fax (510) 528-3444.

Printed in the United States of America

Library of Congress Cataloging-in-Publication Data
Kaye, Beverly L.
    Love 'em or lose 'em : getting good people to stay / Beverly Kaye and
Sharon Jordan-Evans.—3rd ed.
        p.   cm.
    Includes bibliographical references and index.
    ISBN-13: 978-1-57675-327-9
    1. Employee retention.   2. Labor turnover.   I. Jordan-Evans,
Sharon, 1946–   II. Title.
HF5549.5.R58K39   2004
658.3'14—dc22   2004046222
                                                                CIP

Third Edition
10 09 08 07 06 05   10 9 8 7 6 5 4

Interior design: Joan Keyes, Dovetail Publishing Services
Cover design and interior art: Tracy Rocca
Composition: Michael Bass Associates
Editorial services: Michael Bass Associates

To my parents, Mollie and Abe:
Your voices always energize me when I call from the road. Your positive outlook on life and love continues to inspire and amaze me. You've taught me so much.

—Bev

To my grandchildren, Emma, Mackenzie, and Duncan:
You keep teaching me what "love 'em" is really about. I adore you.

—Sharon

Contents

Preface
Love 'Em or Lose 'Em—Talent War Edition
Another Talent War is here—and spreading.

It's predicted to be bigger and longer lasting than the last one.

How will you fare?

When demand outstrips supply, you're in a talent war. When you compete for top talent, steal them from your competitors, and pray they'll stay with you—a little while longer—you're in a talent war. When jobs go unfilled for months, a talent shortage brings productivity to a screeching halt. That's what happened in 1999.

Then, things changed.

The dotcom bubble burst, 9/11 happened, the economy dipped, and unemployment rates rose. Many managers took their eyes off the ball. Instead of focusing on engaging and retaining their good workers, they said, "Quit whining—be glad you have a job." They piled on the work. They removed the perks. They froze the pay. (Of course, the same was done to them.) The result? A demoralized, disengaged workforce. (Surprised?) Recently a Gallup survey found that one-half of the workforce is not engaged, and one in five workers are so negative, they poison the workplace.[1] Now, a new talent war looms.

In the last few years, previously pumped, productive people became disillusioned. They felt disenfranchised and exhausted. They assumed a bunker mentality and withheld their discretionary effort. They quietly hid out, hoping to avoid the axe in the next layoff.

Now, there's another shift under way. This Talent War may make the last war look like a skirmish. What's causing it this time? The confluence of three major factors:

✓ A healthier economy and a brighter job market. That spells more options for good workers.

✓ Unhappy employees, with updated resumés and packed bags. (Eight out of 10 are ready to jump ship at the first sign of greener grass.

✓ Changing demographics. One-half of the 76 million Baby Boomers will be eligible to retire in the next decade. Their replacements will come from a smaller generation. The number of workers between the prime working ages of 25 and 54 will shrink, causing a shortage in skilled workers.

We've dealt with the first two factors before. But we've never seen anything like the demographic earthquake predicted by the pending departure of the Baby Boomers.

Of course, we know that the talent war will affect some industries, geographies, and career functions more than others. For example, many countries already face a nursing shortage of unprecedented proportions, and the problem will only get worse, with aging populations who need more health care. How are things in your backyard? Do you already feel the competition for talent increasing?

Yes, but . . .

There are mitigating factors, and they *could* ease the pain of this Talent War. Fewer workers will be needed as

✓ companies continue to send jobs to other countries (globalization, off-shoring);

✓ technology and productivity advances continue;

✓ skilled workers immigrate from other countries;

✓ some boomers delay their retirement.

No one really knows the effect these factors will have. What we *do* know is this: there will be tremendous upheaval in the workplace as talented people leave to find better jobs or to retire. Fifty-six million jobs will open up between 2002 and 2012.[2] Filling those jobs will require millions of dollars and millions of hours interviewing, orienting, and training replacements. How many of those openings do *you* want to fill?

The Talent War is on. How equipped are you to engage and retain your good people when their options increase and headhunters call? *Love 'Em or Lose 'Em* will help you do just that!

Four Important Words

Readers of our book (this is our third edition) have loved the title *Love 'Em or Lose 'Em: Getting Good People to Stay*. But it's not just a catchy title. The words have important meanings that drive to the heart of our message. Here's how we're using these words:

LOVE   Treat employees fairly and respectfully. Thank them. Challenge and develop them. Care about them and you will engage and retain them.

LOSE   Loss is just as serious when talent retires on the job as when they leave to join a competitor.

GOOD   Consider your solid citizens, not just your high potentials. Stars are people at any level who bring value to the organization.

STAY   Encourage talented employees to stay with the enterprise (if not your own department). Talent will be the key differentiating factor in the competitive battle ahead.

Research Base

Our perspective is based on data collected from numerous industries and organizations. We use exit interview information, focus groups, and the Internet. We (and dozens of helpers) continually scan newspapers, journals, and books.

We ask the question "What kept you?" everywhere.

Our analysis of that data helped us form the original 26 strategies and chapters A–Z. We've continued to build on that original research. We've now met with more than 60,000 managers from large and small companies around the world. We've listened, consulted, provided training, and learned from them. Our "What Kept You" database is continually updated (more than 15,000 respondents by August 2004). All of this helps us refine and expand our engagement and retention strategies.

Now we've distilled those findings into improved retention strategies that give you the crucial competitive edge.

What You'll Find in This Book

We intend *Love 'Em or Lose 'Em* to be both timeless and timely. Timeless in the sense that the suggestions throughout the book should work as well in 1999 (first edition) as in 2020 (we plan to be around!). And timely in the sense that we update the stories, statistics, and workplace views regularly and design them to be relevant for you as a manager *now*.

1. The story of one employee's exit: A.J., our ubiquitous ex-employee (and yes, we mean for you not to know A.J.'s gender, age, or job title), appears in each chapter to let you know how that particular strategy (or lack of it) influenced one individual's decision to leave.
2. Real-life "alas" stories: We've included our own collection of "the fish that got away" stories. These "alas" tales, all true, draw on our combined 40 years of experience in a range of organizations nationally and internationally.
3. Practical "to do" lists: Too many books talk about the "what" and the "why" of retaining and engaging talent. We give you the how-to's!
4. Multiple business examples: In large and small, global and local organizations, these stories reveal what worked to engage and retain talent.
5. Helpful "go to" icons: Most chapters include at least one recommendation of another chapter that builds on a key point. This allows you to skip around to find the ideas that are most relevant and important to you.
6. A quick retention/engagement index (REI): In the Zenith chapter, you'll find ways to assess your current retention/engagement focus. Go there first if you want to learn where you stand. Or read it after the rest of the book to see what you've learned or to find your next focus.

7. A "troubleshooting guide" appears at the end. Managers around the globe, from CEOs to supervisors, tell us about their talent troubles. They describe their retention and engagement dilemmas, and ask for our take. Our format offers a paragraph about the problem, a question from a manager, and our "Dear Abby"–like response. Check it out.

Double-click on These Three Truths

Three key messages recur throughout the chapters. They're basic and retention-critical. If you're a senior leader, drive them. If you manage others, implement them.

Truth 1: Engaging and Keeping Good People Is a Perennial Issue

Savvy managers realize they need their best people to stay, regardless of economic lane changes. "Stay": your talent has not just checked in but is tuned in and turned on as well. They are engaged in the business of the business. Engagement and retention are two sides of the same coin. This book teaches how to do both.

Truth 2: The Manager Has Influence

Many managers claim no responsibility for employee engagement and retention. They believe retention is largely about money, perks, and benefits—areas where they have little control. We know that is not true. In addition to fair pay, people want

- challenging, meaningful work,
- a chance to learn and grow,
- great co-workers,
- recognition and respect, and
- a good boss.

The manager can influence these factors. Senior leadership and organizational policies matter, too, and so do your employees, who also have to take responsibility for their own satisfaction (Give them *Love It,*

Don't Leave It: 26 Ways to Get What You Want at Work, Berret-Koehler, 2003). But this is about you. You are crucial to engaging and retaining good people.

Truth 3: There Are 26 Tested Strategies You Can Use to Engage and Retain Your Talent

Most managers want to do a great job engaging and keeping their good people—why wouldn't they? But all managers (yes, even the best) could improve. *Love 'Em or Lose 'Em* does not offer a single technique or a large, complex program for keeping good people. Instead, it provides 26 choices. Each includes dozens of small, easy-to-implement ideas. You pick your favorite—then do it.

Make This Yours

We wrote *Love 'Em or Lose 'Em* to make your life easier. To help you in a real-time, day-to-day way. We wrote it because you make such an impact on the lives of your workforce. That's an awesome responsibility that deserves all the help and support it can get.

✓ Use this as your guidebook—as you would a vehicle maintenance manual.
✓ Return to it again and again.
✓ Dog-ear the page corners.
✓ Use a highlighter on what matters most to you.
✓ Put a bookmark in key chapters, and leave the book on your own manager's desk!
✓ Personally commit to implementing just one chapter.

Remember, your attention to retention is critical. You know who your stars are—the ones you cannot afford to lose. They are your talented, committed employees—"high potentials" and solid citizens alike. You love them because they are critical to your success. They are the heart and soul of your organization. And your competitors want them!

Acknowledgments

Our first thank you goes to the many line managers from around the world who devote considerable energy to engaging and retaining their talent. They've shared their outcomes, given us ideas, and helped us size up the current and developing situation. Their questions, comments, and concerns helped us decide to write this third edition—and we thank them for that. We hope it will help them stay ahead of the curve on the vital issues of retention and engagement.

We sought the wisdom of our publisher, Steve Piersanti, about the timing for this edition, and he agreed the time is now. We are deeply grateful to him for sending notes of appreciation, making time to debate with us about our concepts, and involving us so completely in every decision surrounding the book. Our heartfelt appreciation goes out to Steve and the entire Berrett-Koehler team.

We thank the internal human resources practitioners and leaders with whom we work for feedback they've given and the innumerable ways they've tested and applied our materials. We greatly appreciate Career Systems and the wonderful trainers and consultants who help us deliver the "Love 'Em" message globally. They keep us current and continually challenged to make our workshops and learning tools "deceptively simple and delightfully engaging." The CSI sales team and support team push us to stay "deliberately flexible" so that these ideas are used and useful to busy managers everywhere.

Sandy LoSchiavo and Lorianne Speaks helped us gather the latest research and spent long hours typing and proofing. Nancy Breuer

(WorkPositive) and Tracy Rocca have been with us since the beginning. Nancy once more made sure our distinct voices blended properly, and Tracy applied her artistic magic.

Our own home teams also came through for us, as they always do. Bev thanks Lindsey for making her laugh by constantly poking fun at our alphabet! And she thanks Barry for putting up with yet another weekend devoted to work. Sharon thanks her kids and grandkids for their love and support. And she thanks Mike for reading another draft and cooking another dinner.

We certainly have learned to appreciate one another even more. Each time our work together gets smoother. We've learned to know what draws a groan from the other and what produces the response "Awesome!"

We continue to love our work (we hope it shows) and appreciate all who support us (we hope we show it!). Thank you.

Introduction

I quit.
I'm giving you my notice.
I found another opportunity.
I've accepted another offer.
Can we talk?

If any of the above strikes fear in your heart or makes your stomach sink, you are not alone. Anyone managing or supervising others, whether in a skyscraper, a coffee shop, or a volunteer group, reacts with dismay to statements like these—especially when the people saying them are critical to your team.

By "critical," we don't mean just your top performers or your "high potentials." We mean the "solid citizens" too—those who show up day after day to reliably do their work. They are necessary to the success of your unit and your peace of mind. They are the steady, dependable employees whom you simply cannot afford to lose. They are your stars.

Like A.J.—a critical and solid performer making a competitive salary and working for an organization that has a good future. On the next page, you'll find the exit memo from A.J. to the department manager and the manager's manager.

Read it. Underline the points that resonate. Could this happen to you?

INTEROFFICE MEMO

To: Carlos and Madeleine
From: A.J.
Re: Exit Interview

Today I received the Exit Interview form from Human Resources. I put the form aside. It didn't ask the right questions for me, so I'm writing this letter instead. I still feel bad about leaving our company. I liked working with you and our team. I just couldn't stay. Maybe my letter will help you to prevent this from happening again.

Carlos, I think you are an effective manager. You complete projects, achieve goals, and accomplish everything through a talented group of employees. All of these were rewarding while I was still learning our business. Unfortunately, you got too busy to pay attention to the little things—like saying good morning. Or trying to delegate assignments so that we could learn something new. Instead, under pressure, you always took the short-cut and gave the work to people who had experience. How can anyone grow if they don't have a chance to learn? We talked a few times about the chance for me to attend training classes or to prepare and present our plan to the executives, but those chances never materialized. A year later, I began to understand that they never would happen.

Madeleine, I have always admired you. You provide great leadership and direction to Carlos and our team and our colleagues in the division. When I first joined the company four years ago, I was so impressed by our mission statement and corporate values. I hoped to have a long and happy career here.

I have to say I became disillusioned and disengaged over time. I really decided to leave in the last two months. We worked so hard on that last project. I rescheduled my vacation. The whole team put in extra hours. We produced quality work on time, achieving all objectives. Then the company decided not to implement the plan. I could even understand that decision, knowing how fast change happens here and in any business. But no one took the time to let us know. We continued with implementation for three weeks before we heard the rumors that the project was canceled. We would have understood if you'd come to our area and told us. Instead we were angry and disappointed.

It is true that my new position pays a higher salary, but I'm not leaving for money. I need to work in a place where I can make a contribution and people treat each other with respect. Sadly, my work didn't seem to make a difference here.

Thank you for all you taught me. Please remember that thoughtful planning, honest and continuous communication, and basic human respect go a long way with your employees.

I wish you every success.

Have you ever had an employee like A.J.? A solid contributor, someone you really could not afford to lose, but who left anyway? How many times have you said:

"If I'd only known."

"Why didn't they tell me?"

"Why didn't I see that coming?"

"The answer was easy. I could have fixed that."

"Why didn't I ask?"

Some frustrated disappointed employees could do worse than leave you. They might quit and stay.

Managers ask us how they can prevent both kinds of employee losses. We suggest scanning the 26 chapters in this book. Pick out a few that capture you because you have a hunch they relate directly to you or to one of your people.

And if you have no idea what would really keep your talent, then start with chapter 1, Ask: What Keeps You?

And if you're not convinced that this problem is in your area of responsibility, then read chapter 2, Buck: It Stops Here.

Ask

What Keeps You?

They never asked. —A.J.

Why do we ask great questions in exit interviews but neglect asking early enough to make a difference? Instead, we brainstorm. Human resource specialists and senior-level leaders ponder the question. Special task forces and consultants conduct research. They benchmark other organizations in related industries, all in a quest for the answer. Eventually, they create *the* strategy, *the* master plan. What are they trying to do? Engage and hold on to key talent—the employees, knowledge workers, associates, and technical or functional specialists who do the work and keep your company successful.

All that effort, time, and money may be well spent. But we have noticed that the obvious is often overlooked. Have *you* ever asked your employees what keeps them at your company or what might entice them away? If not, why not?

Ask—So You Don't Have to Guess

When we suggest asking employees why they stay or what would keep them, we hear, "You've got to be kidding," "Isn't that illegal?" or "What if they give me an answer I don't want to hear?" We dance around this core subject usually for one of three reasons:

✓ Some managers fear putting people on the spot or putting ideas into their heads (as if they never thought about leaving on their own).

✓ Some managers are afraid they will be unable to do anything anyway, so why ask? They fear that the question will raise more dust than they can settle and may cause employees to expect answers and solutions that are out of the managers' hands.

✓ Some managers say they don't have the time to have these critical one-on-one discussions with their talented people. There is an urgency to produce, leaving little time to listen, let alone ask. If you don't have time for these discussions with the people who contribute to your success, where will you find the time to interview, select, orient, and train their replacements?

The Dangers of Guessing

What if you don't ask? What if you just keep trying to guess what Tara or Mike or Marilyn really want? You will guess right sometimes. The

Alas

A senior manager told us of an employee who was leaving his company. On her last day, the senior manager, who was upset at the loss, expressed his disappointment that she was leaving. He wished her well but said, "I wish there were something we could have done to keep you," assuming that her direct supervisor has asked what would make her stay. But the supervisor hadn't asked, and something could have been done. The employee said she would have stayed if she could have been more involved in some of the new task forces, as she felt the participation was vital to her goal of growing her career. It was a request that would have been easy to fill—if only he had known!

year-end bonus might please them all. Money can inspire loyalty and commitment for the near term. But if the key to retaining Tara is to give her a chance to learn something new, whereas Mike wants to telecommute, how could you ever guess that? Ask—so you don't have to guess.

Asking has positive side effects. The person you ask will feel cared about, valued, and important. Many times that leads to stronger loyalty and commitment to you and the organization. In other words, just asking the question is a retention strategy.

How to Ask

How and when do you bring up this topic? How can you increase the odds of getting honest input from your employees? There is no single way or time to ask. It could happen during a developmental or career discussion with your employees. (You do hold those, don't you?) Or you may schedule a meeting with your valued employees for the express purpose of finding out what will keep them. One manager sent the following invitation to give his key people some time to think and to prepare for the conversation:

YOU ARE INVITED TO ATTEND

The next step in your continued development.

You make a difference and I value your contributions.

Let's discuss some things that are important to you and me:

What will keep you here?

What might entice you away?

What is most energizing about your work?

Are we fully utilizing your talents?

What is inhibiting your success?

What can I do differently to best assist you?

Please schedule a meeting with me within the next two weeks to discuss this and anything else you'd like to talk about.

Regardless of when you start this dialogue, remember to set the context by telling your employees how critical they are to you and your team and how important it is to you that they stay. Then find out what will keep them. Listen carefully to their responses.

He Dared to Ask

Charlie set up a meeting with his plant manager, Ken, for Monday morning. After some brief conversation about the weekend activities, Charlie said, "Ken, you are critical to me and to this organization. I'm not sure I've told you that directly or often enough. But you are. I can't imagine losing you. So, I'd like to know what will keep you here. And what might entice you away?"

Ken was a bit taken aback—but felt flattered. He thought for a moment and then said, "You know, I aspire to move up in the organization at some point, and I'd love to have some exposure to the senior team. I'd like to see how they operate—and frankly I'd like them to get to know me too." Charlie responded, "I could take you with me to some senior staff meetings. Would that be a start?" Ken said, "That would be great."

Charlie delivered on Ken's request one week later.

What If—

What If You Can't Give What They Want?

Most managers don't ask because they fear one of two responses: a raise or a promotion. Let's look at another possible discussion between Charlie and Ken.

Following Charlie's question about what will keep him, Ken replied immediately, "A 20 percent raise will do it!" Now, some managers will say things like, "Are you kidding? You're already at the top of your pay range." That response shuts down the dialogue and makes a key employee feel less than key. Charlie was ready for this possibility, though, and said to Ken, "You are worth that and more to me. I'd love to say yes, but I will need to investigate the possibility. I'm honestly not sure what I can do immediately, but I'll come back to you by next week with some answers and a possible timeline for a raise. Meanwhile, what else matters to you? What else are you hoping for?" Ken responded with his interest in getting to know the senior team—and Charlie was ready to act on that one instantly.

Research shows clearly that people want more from work than just a paycheck. When you ask the question "What else?" we guarantee there will be at least one thing your talented employee wants that you can give. Remember to listen actively as your employees talk about what will keep them on your team or in your organization.

see UNDERSTAND

What If You Ask What They Want and They Say, "I Don't Know"?

Remember that this is not an interrogation or a test. It's okay not to know. Some people will be surprised by your questioning and need some time to think about it. Let them think, schedule another meeting, and set the stage for an ongoing dialogue about your employees' wants, needs, and career goals. Engaging and keeping your talent is a process, not an event.

What If They Don't Trust You Enough to Answer Honestly?

Discussions like these require trust. If your employees are afraid to answer your questions for any reason, you may need to build trust with them before you can expect honest, heartfelt responses. Try to discover why trust is missing in the relationship, and purposely act in trust-building ways. Seek help from colleagues, human resource professionals, or coaches.

What If They Question Your Motivation or Smile and Say, "What Book Did You Last Read?"

Be honest. If you're not in the habit of having dialogues like these, it will feel strange—for you and perhaps for them. Tell them you *did* read a book or attend a course about retaining talent, and you did it because they matter to you. Tell them you honestly want to hear their answers and you want to partner with them to help them get what they want and need.

TO DO . . .

✓ Ask each employee what will keep him or her at your company or your department.

✓ Make a card or note in your computer for every employee's answer.

✓ Every month, review the cards or notes and ask yourself what you've done for that employee that relates to his or her needs.

Why Most Say They Stay

We've asked over 15,000 people why they stayed in an organization for "a while" (yes, it's a relative term). Our findings confirm what many others have learned about the most common reasons employees remain at a company (and what will help retain them). The items come up again and again throughout every industry and at every level. The differences between functions, levels, genders, and ages are minor. Here are the top 20 responses listed in order of frequency as of August 2004 (Note: 91 percent of respondents listed at least one of the first two items among the top few reasons they stayed, and they all listed at least one of the first three):

1. Exciting work and challenge
2. Career growth, learning, and development
3. Working with great people
4. Fair pay
5. Supportive management/good boss
6. Being recognized, valued, and respected
7. Benefits
8. Meaningful work and making a difference

9. Pride in the organization, its mission, and its product
10. Great work environment and culture
11. Autonomy, creativity, and sense of control
12. Flexibility: work hours, dress, and so on
13. Location
14. Job security and stability
15. Diverse, changing work assignments
16. Fun on the job
17. Being part of a team
18. Responsibility
19. Loyalty, commitment to the organization or coworkers
20. Inspiring leadership

How do your employees' answers compare with the list? Find out what truly matters to them by asking. Then create customized, innovative approaches to retaining your talent.

By the way, if you'd like to see the complete "What Kept You" survey data, including multiple demographic breakdowns, go to our Web site, www.keepem.com.

A Word about Pay

Some of you immediately zeroed in on the fact that fair pay lands in fourth place on this list. Here is what we know about pay. If it is seen as noncompetitive, unfair, or simply insufficient to sustain life, it will be a large dissatisfier. Your talented people will become vulnerable to talent theft or will begin looking around for something better, especially in a favorable job market. But here's the rub. While it can be a huge dissatisfier if inadequate, it won't keep people who are unhappy in other key areas.

So if your talented people are not being challenged, or grown, or cared about, a big paycheck will not keep them for long. Researchers throughout the years have found this to be true. One named Herzberg found in the 1950s that pay is a "hygiene factor"—make sure it's there or it will be noticed![3] So, do what you can as a manager to influence your organization's compensation programs. Be sure they are competitive and fair—then focus on *what else* you can do to keep your talent.

TO DO . . .

✓ Look back at the list of reasons people stay and ask yourself which of these you can influence.

✓ Check all those that you believe are largely within your control. If our hunch is correct, you will find that you can influence many more than you may have thought.

Beyond "Why Did You Stay?"

Most of this chapter focuses on the questions "What keeps you?" and "What might entice you away?" But there are many other questions you might ask to try to engage and keep your employees.

If you think you have retention headaches, Commander Abrashoff of the U.S. Navy talked in a Harvard Business Review *article about the difficulties he faced when he took command of the USS* Benfold *and found that his sailors were extremely dissatisfied.[4] The commander asked every sailor on his ship the following questions:*

- *Where are you from?*
- *Why did you join the navy?*
- *What's your family situation?*
- *Is there anything the navy can do to help your family?*
- *What do you like most about the* Benfold?
- *What do you like least?*
- *What would you change if you could?*

"Getting to know my crew as individuals did more than generate innovations and process improvements. It was also an important discipline for me. Getting to know someone as an individual prevents

you from zoning out when they're talking. It forces you to listen. You can't ignore or shut down people you know and respect." He also learned to listen to what they had to say.

"I don't like to admit this, but listening doesn't come naturally to me. I often just pretended to hear people. How many times, I asked myself, had I barely glanced up from my work when a subordinate came in my office? I wasn't listening. I was marking time until it was my turn to give orders."

Many of our first-time readers told us they took our "ask" ideas to new places. Here are a few of them:

At Orientation

One large medical center decided to demand that managers "ask" immediately after bringing in new employees. Their employee orientation manual states the following:

✓ Find out from new employees what motivates them and what will make them stay on the job.
✓ Begin getting to know them as individuals.
✓ Ask questions about what is important to them and why they accepted the position.
✓ Ask them to tell you the work they feel they are best at, what they most enjoy doing, what they value, what they need to learn to work at their best, and the results they feel they can be expected to deliver.
✓ Show respect for their previous experiences and encourage them to provide insight and suggestions from their fresh perspectives.

During Performance Appraisals

The CEO of a large medical facility decided to supplement the performance appraisal system with a series of "ask" questions. He distributed the questions to all his direct reports, who were required to fill in the questionnaire before the appraisal meeting. One of his key employees said to us, "This was the best discussion I've had in 20 years." Here are the questions:

✓ What makes for a great day?
✓ What can we do to make your job more satisfying?
✓ What can we do to support your career goals?
✓ Do you get enough recognition?
✓ What can we do to keep you here?

At the Start of Each Quarter

An engineering organization has invented its own "non-touchy-feely" way to ask. Some engineering managers put the question this way:

"I'm gathering data on what it would take to maintain your longevity over time. Can you provide some data points that are important to you and their projected financial requirements?"

The engineering managers in this company built spreadsheets, listing the requirements of each of their direct reports, computed the overall cost, and submitted them for approval through their own chain of command. Approximately 75 percent of each spreadsheet submitted was approved.

As Part of a "Stay" Interview

Leaders of a large financial organization asked all managers to hold "stay" interviews with all the people on their teams. They recommended 20 minutes and suggested these interviews become part of the regular monthly one-on-ones. Here are a few of the questions:

✓ What about your job makes you jump out of bed in the morning?
✓ What makes you hit the snooze button?
✓ If you were to win the lottery and resign, what would you miss the most?
✓ What would be the one thing that, if it changed in your current role, would make you consider moving on?
✓ If you had a magic wand, what would be the one thing you would change about this department?
✓ If you had to go back to a position in your past and stay for an extended period of time, which one would it be and why?

Let these ideas serve as catalysts for your own thinking. Create a list of your favorite questions. Ask them of your talented people. And ask again, listen carefully, and customize your retention efforts.

Retention is essentially an individual activity, not a group activity.

BOTTOM LINE

Stop guessing what will keep your stars home and happy. Gather your courage and try this with the employees you want to keep. Set aside time to start the dialogue. Don't guess and don't assume they all want the same thing (like pay or promotion). Schedule another meeting if they need to think about it for a while.

This may be the most important strategy in this book. Asking will not only make your talented people feel valued, but their answers will provide the information you need to customize strategies to keep each of them.

It doesn't matter so much where, when, or how you ask—just ASK!

Chapter 2

It Stops Here

I think my manager actually could have kept me. But I don't think he ever saw it as his job.

—A.J.

When we ask supervisors and managers how to keep good people, many immediately respond, "With money." Research suggests that 89 percent of managers truly believe it's largely about the money.[5] These managers place the responsibility for keeping key people squarely in the hands of senior management. They blame organizational policies or pay scales for the loss of talent. Or they point the finger at the competition or the location. It's always someone else's fault.

Well, the truth is, *you matter most.* If you are a manager at any level, a frontline supervisor, or a project leader, you actually have more power than anyone else to keep your best employees. Why? Because the factors that drive employee satisfaction, engagement, and commitment are largely within your control. And the factors that satisfy and engage employees are the ones that keep them on your team. Those factors haven't changed much over the past 25 years. Many researchers who have studied retention agree on what engages or satisfies people and therefore influences them to stay: meaningful and challenging work, a

see ASK

16

chance to learn and grow, fair and competitive compensation, great coworkers, recognition, respect, and a good boss.[6] Don't you want those things?

Alas

There's nothing I can do about our brain drain. The competition is offering more money and better perks. We don't stand a chance.
—Manager, retail pharmacy

You *do* stand a chance. Your relationship with employees is key to their satisfaction and decisions to stay or leave. Consider this:

✓ One study found that 50 percent of work satisfaction is determined by the relationship a worker has with his or her immediate boss.[7]

✓ Interviews conducted by the Saratoga Institute with 20,000 workers who had just left an employer revealed that the supervisor's behavior was the main reason people quit.[8]

✓ A 25-year-long Gallup Organization study based on interviews with 12 million workers at 7,000 companies also found that the relationship with a manager largely determines the length of an employee's stay.[9]

✓ Research by the Corporate Leadership Council found that a high quality manager is of *standout importance* in attracting and retaining key talent.[10]

✓ Research by the authors (over 15,000 respondents) found that most retention factors are within managers' *influence*.

In other words, *you matter.*

People are our greatest resource. We are "caring" already, but we need to do more . . . really step out of the box. We need to give our undivided attention, day in and day out, to our people and our talent . . . we are too easily distracted. How much of our day is spent on products and pricing versus people? YOU [managers] set the example. Our best resource is not in our vault; it is in our people, and we can't lock them up . . . they walk out the door everyday. I want us to be a magnet for those people, drawing them back.

—EVP, large national bank

It's Up to You

A good boss who cares about keeping good employees will help them find what they want from their workplace. We're not saying you carry this responsibility alone. Senior management and your organization's policies, systems, and culture have an impact on your ability to keep talented people. You may have human resources professionals who can help support your efforts. Yet, because of what research tells us about *why* people leave their jobs and organizations, you still have the greatest power (and responsibility) for keeping your talented employees.

Insofar as employee commitment exists, it is to the boss, to the team, and to the project. That's different from loyalty, which previously was to the name on the building or to the brand. Therefore, any retention strategy must be driven by individual managers and supervisors, not just the folks in human resources.

—President, Aon Consulting Institute

On the Line

Most of you are in charge of certain assets. You are held accountable for protecting those assets and for growing them. Today, your most critical assets are *people,* not *property.* Outstanding people give you and your organization a competitive advantage. Regardless of the job market, you no doubt want to hold on to your best.

Are you accountable for selecting and keeping talented people? We have heard of a CEO who charged $30,000 to a manager's operating budget because he needlessly lost a talented person. The buck really did stop there!

> *In a 2001 letter to shareholders, Jack Welch, CEO of General Electric, said that an organization's key employees should be loved, nurtured, and rewarded in the soul and wallet because they are the ones who make magic happen. He went on to say that losing one of these people must be held up as a leadership sin—a real failing.*

We're not suggesting that managers be punished when their people are promoted or move on to learn something new. You will inevitably lose some talented employees occasionally, especially as they pursue their career dreams. But we do recommend that managers be held accountable for being *good managers* and for creating a retention culture where people feel motivated, cared about, and rewarded.

Calling All Managers of Managers

If managers report to you, do you hold them accountable for the teams they manage? How? You've probably heard the maxim that busy people do what is *inspected,* not necessarily what is *expected.* You can expect—and should find ways to inspect—honest efforts to keep good people, because those people build your business. Here are some options.

TO DO . . .

Devise a Retention Commitment Process:

✓ List all 26 strategies in this book (use the table of contents as a summary) on a paper or electronic form. Or have your team narrow the 26 down to 10 or so that they think are the most appropriate for your culture. Ask each of your managers or supervisors to commit to two they are willing to implement within the next six months. Have them circle and initial those two and return a copy of the form to you.

✓ Six months later, ask them to return their retention commitment forms to you with a description of what they did for each of the strategies to which they committed.

✓ Check in and check up on your managers. Set a performance goal of increasing retention by a specific percentage over the previous year.

✓ Rate your managers against the goal, and reward them accordingly. Spotlight your top retention managers, just as you would your most productive or innovative managers. And remember, positive reinforcement works better than negative!

✓ Courageously coach and manage the managers who chase talent out the back door. If they can't or won't change, help them leave the job or the organization.

✓ Send a note to managers. Tape it to the front of this book. Hold a meeting in two weeks and talk about their reactions. Here is a sample memo:

Who is responsible for making retention happen? Is it HR? No. HR builds the framework. Is it senior management? Senior management provides the resources and the direction. Who is responsible? We all are! We all have to make retention come to life. Your own people frame their perceptions of this company by your behavior. To them, you are the company. They came here because of you. They stay here because of you, and 75 percent of those who quit don't quit the company—they quit their managers.

—COO, financial services organization

✓ Model what you want them to do. Tell your direct reports what retention strategies you're working on (after you've asked what they want), and then really work on those strategies. Remember that your actions speak much more loudly than your words.

If you're not a manager of managers, hold yourself accountable. Look at the talented people you are responsible for engaging and for keeping in the organization. Decide which strategies in this book you could use right away to increase the odds that they will stay.

So They Go

So what? Can't you just replace them? You might be able to replace your key people, but at what cost? Most retention experts agree that replacing key talent will cost you two times their annual salaries. And replacing "platinum" workers (those with specialized skills) will run four to five times their annual salary.

see NUMBERS

Even if you can afford to replace them, will you be able to find talented replacements?

> *You think 1999 was a bad time to be hiring? That year was only a footprint for what we'll see in 2008. We'll be facing the worst labor shortage in our lifetime within the next five years.*
>
> —Jeff Taylor, founder, Monster

The demographers and workforce pundits disagree. Will we be short 3 million or 10 million workers by 2010? And what about 2012? The mitigating factors (globalization/offshoring, technology advances, delayed retirement, immigration) are so many and so mathematically complex that some feel a crystal ball would do as good a job as the experts when it comes to projecting the actual number.

What we do know is this: We'll have approximately 56 million jobs open between 2002 and 2012.[11] Twenty-two million of those represent new jobs, due to a growing economy (3 percent annually on average). The remaining 34 million jobs will be available because people leave them. Many of those job leavers are baby boomers, born between 1946 and 1964. Approximately half of them will be eligible to retire in the next decade. Anthony Carnevale, former chairman of the National Commission for Employment Policy, has warned that the demographic shortfall in labor will make the talent war of the late 1990s seem like a minor irritation.

TO DO . . .

✓ Pay attention to the research about what keeps people. Note that most of the proven strategies are within your control.

✓ If you manage managers, hold them accountable for hiring and keeping good people in the organization. Establish clear expectations, and measure results.

✓ Do just one thing. Choose a chapter in this book and try a strategy. See how it works. Modify and adapt it to fit your needs. Then try another.

BOTTOM LINE

The retention buck really does stop with you. We are not ignoring the impact of senior management, organization policies, and individual employees' attitudes and actions. But we know you have great power to influence your talented employees' decisions about staying. Show that you care about them and their needs. Remember them. Notice them. Listen to them. Thank them. Love them or lose them.

Chapter 3

CAREERS

Support Growth

I guess I just never saw a future for myself here. I don't mean I ever expected a path all laid out, but I did expect that somewhere, someone would talk to me about my future.

—A.J.

A.J. probably had a future with this employer, but if that future was a secret in senior managers' minds only, it had no power to influence A.J.'s decisions. If there has never been a discussion about an employee's career, your chances of keeping that person engaged or with you are greatly diminished.

In fact, far too many managers steer clear of career conversations. Which of the following barriers keep you from opening up this topic?

✓ No one, let alone me, knows what the future holds.
✓ It is just not the right time.
✓ I'm not prepared.
✓ I wouldn't know what to say.
✓ We've just reorganized. It will be a while before anyone knows anything about career possibilities.

✓ I would never open something I couldn't close.

✓ I don't know enough about what's outside my department to offer advice.

✓ I don't want anyone blaming me if they don't get what they want.

✓ Why should I help? Nobody ever helped me.

What your employees really want are two-way conversations with you to talk about their abilities, choices, and ideas. They want you to listen. They may not expect you to have the answers, but they expect and really want to have the dialogue.

You construct the pipeline for the flow of talent in your organization. When your people feel that you care about developing them, they believe the organization cares.

> When I look at the wonderful people who work with me in my department, and the many, many talents they possess, I can do nothing short of helping them become better and better. I am privileged to be in a position to encourage their growth . . . and when they grow, I feel blessed that I somehow played a small part.
>
> —Barbara Pattison, director, Surgical Services, PBCH

This chapter provides the basics on building your talent pipeline. Five steps you can take routinely will support your employees' search for a good career fit.[12]

Step 1	**Know Their Talents**
Step 2	**Offer Your Perspective**
Step 3	**Discuss Trends**
Step 4	**Discover Multiple Options**
Step 5	**Codesign an Action Plan**

Step 1: Know Their Talents

The primary objective of career conversations is gathering information that will tell you more about your employees. It is frequently difficult for employees to talk about their skills, values, and interests. Open up a dialogue that gives you and your employees an opportunity to become more aware of who they are both professionally and personally.

To get them talking, ask questions that help them to think more deeply about their unique skills, interests, and values. The toughest part is to listen while they answer, as a diligent researcher would. Probe, inquire, and discover more.

see UNDERSTAND

TO DO . . .

Try asking these questions, and then probe each answer more deeply:

✓ What makes you unique in this organization?
✓ Tell me about an accomplishment of which you are particularly proud.
✓ What are your most important work-related values? Which values are met and not met at work?
✓ If you had to choose among working with people, data, things, or ideas, which mixture would make you the happiest? Why?

Step 2: Offer Your Perspective

Helping your employees to reflect on their own reputations, on the feedback they've gotten from others, and on the areas they need to develop is essential. Your frequent feedback is critical.

Think back to the last performance review you gave. It probably was based on past performance and connected to that employee's raise. Development feedback is different. It is future oriented and focused on areas where the employee can improve.

Employees want specific feedback with examples of their performance and the effect on their future goals. Have them seek out people in their career audience at all levels who will give them a more realistic self-portrait to help them develop faster and smarter.

see TRUTH

Alas (almost)

Recently, a senior HR person stopped to say hi to someone who started on the same day she did—about six months earlier. He was considered a fast-track high-potential and was getting excellent press from very high up in the organization. She said, "Hi, how's it going?" He shrugged his shoulders and said it was going okay, he guessed, but he wasn't really happy and didn't feel he was making any progress. She was shocked to find that no one had ever told this guy what a great job he was doing. When she told him who was impressed by him, his face lit up. He had no idea he was valued.

TO DO . . .

Try preparing for these conversations by asking yourself these questions:

✓ Which tasks do they most need to focus on to maximize their contributions?

✓ How do you really see their potential to grow based on what you identified on their most recent performance appraisals?

✓ What are their reputations among coworkers?

✓ How will you begin this conversation?

Think about all the awkward conversations you've had with employees whose career goals are simply out of sync with reality given their strengths and weaknesses. Remember, *the absence of honest feedback kept them out of sync!* Employees continually tell us that they want straight talk. Want to keep them? Level with them.

Step 3: Discuss Trends

Helping your people consider their options means helping them look beyond your department to detect shifts and changes that might impact their careers. You will need to sniff out your company's growth areas and limitations as well as changes in the skills the industry will require.

Alas

Lenore was exactly what our organization needed. She was young and wanted to use her technical as well as managerial skills, wanted to develop business, and in fact had already brought some in. She decided to look for a new job when she heard that there were some changes coming in our organization, and she realized she didn't know what would happen to her. She said that her first manager was great at coaching and keeping her in the loop, but that she had recently been moved to work for another manager who had shown no interest in her career. So with the threat of impending change, and a manager who didn't seem to care, she took an offer at a small start-up company. She was clear that it was not the salary and benefits that drew her. It was the hope of a better manager, one who would keep her "in the loop" and care about her career. The exit interview lasted 90 minutes. I asked her if she would reconsider. She declined.

—Human resources manager

Clearly, a good career conversation with her new manager could have influenced Lenore's decision to look around.

TO DO . . .

Ask yourself if your employees know the following points regarding trends:

✓ The major economic, political, and social changes taking place that will have the greatest effect on your organization

✓ The opportunities and problems ahead

✓ What areas are changing the most within your industry

✓ How their profession will be different in the next two to five years
✓ What really counts for success in your organization
✓ Which trade publications, journals, and organization newsletters provide information on industry and business trends

---

You don't have to take this all on your own shoulders. But you do have to ensure that your employees know what's going on in your organization. By suggesting others who can provide additional perspectives on these and other issues, you open channels for your employees and give them a closer look at the key business needs of the organization. Have you done this lately?

Step 4: Discover Multiple Options

Helping your employees consider multiple career goals while they grow within their current positions is a key element in development. When employees analyze their potential development goals in terms of business needs and the strategic intent of the organization, everyone wins. Caution! The employee is still primarily responsible for his or her career. Our suggestions do not mean *telling* the person what to do. Instead, offer choices for employees to analyze and consider.

see GOALS

This is important, but sometimes difficult. For generations, the only acceptable career direction has been up. But there are at least five other ways employees can move their careers along. You can help your employees consider options like these:

1. Moving laterally (a change in job, but not necessarily a change in the level of responsibility)
2. Exploring (requires answering questions like "What else can I do?")
3. Enriching (seeds the current job with more chances to learn and grow)
4. Realigning (reconciles the demands of work with other priorities, or readies them for another area)
5. Relocating (yes, leaving the organization if the work simply cannot match a person's skills, interests, or values)

You can give your employees permission to discover the possibilities based on what turns them on, what they value, and what they can contribute to the organization.

The more career goals your employee identifies, the better. *The biggest career frustrations (and the most exits) occur when an employee's only goal is thwarted.*

TO DO ...

Ask your employees these questions. All are critical to goal setting:

✓ Do you have enough information about the organization's current activities and plans to select several career goals?
✓ How can you get the information you need?
✓ Have you considered all available directions in selecting your career options?
✓ Do your options adequately cover a variety of scenarios?
✓ Should you select more career options?
✓ Are your goals compatible with organizational goals and plans?

Once you have helped your employees look at options so that all their plans are not caught up in the vertical mind-set, they will feel as if they have more leverage to manage their own careers.

Step 5: Codesign an Action Plan

Codesigning increases your commitment and the employee's commitment to the plan. Consider all of the steps the employee would have to take to realize the best choices in Step 4. Develop contingency plans for each. Then, if one is blocked, the other paths will already be laid out.

Help your employees to identify the obstacles to each path. Then brainstorm ways around the obstacles. During the process, help them to remember and maximize the assets they already have.

TO DO ...

Try asking any or all of these questions. The answers form the action plan:

✓ What skills would you need to gain to help you achieve your goals?
✓ What abilities do you already possess that would help you toward any of your targets?
✓ Who is in your network already who might open a door for you?
✓ What training could I make available to fill the gaps you see?
✓ What kinds of on-the-job development could help you move closer to several of your options?

Remember, your job is to stimulate your employees into identifying skills, development opportunities, and knowledge areas required for each alternative. Your job is not to build their plans, but to support them!

Career Discussion Do's and Don'ts

Know Their Talents

- Do draw individuals out and find out what makes them "tick."
- Do give encouragement and support.
- Do ask open-ended, probing questions, using words like *what*, *where*, and *when*.

- Don't take your employees for granted.
- Don't interrogate your employees—investigate.
- Don't tell your employees what to do—listen for what they want to do.

Offer Your Perspective

- Do ask individuals to assess themselves and ask others for their perspectives.

- Don't say things that aren't true just to avoid confrontation.

- Do give specific, concrete, constructive feedback with examples.
- Do clarify standards and expectations.

- Don't just focus on performance feedback—use developmental feedback also.
- Don't emphasize weaknesses only. Be balanced and leverage strengths as well.

Discuss Trends

- Do provide information on organization, industry, and professional trends.
- Do allow talented individuals to access your network.
- Do discuss your perspective on how current challenges may affect their careers.

- Don't underestimate the impact of constant change on employees' development.
- Don't avoid talking about an unpredictable future.
- Don't sidestep the importance of how company culture (unwritten norms) can derail careers.

Discover Multiple Options

- Do discuss multiple, realistic career goals.
- Do encourage individuals to envision their future.
- Do help set goals that are aligned with business needs.

- Don't let individuals pursue vertical moves only.
- Don't make promises.
- Don't forget to plan for several possible outcomes.

Codesign an Action Plan

- Do suggest resources and on-the-job activities.
- Do get individuals to take action.
- Do be direct to help strengthen their plans.

- Don't depend on training alone for development.
- Don't steer clear of recommending sources outside of your department.
- Don't ignore the current assignment as a great practice field.

BOTTOM LINE

Keeping your employees on a continual path of growing, developing, and adding new skills will help you keep your competitive edge. You must help them discover the inevitable barriers that will get in their way. But they must overcome them and do the work. Help them build alliances and relationships to meet their goals.

Any organization that ignores the ambitions of good people can't expect to keep them.

Chapter 4

IGNITY

Show Respect

I generally felt respected in this organization, but that was not the case for everyone. I remember feeling embarrassed when a manager humiliated his administrative assistant in front of several of her colleagues. It was so disrespectful, and no one said or did anything about it.

—A.J.

What kind of boss would your employees say you are? Would they say that you are smart, dedicated, motivating, hard-charging? How about results oriented, demanding, or fun to work with? Just as you tolerate a range of behaviors from your employees, so too your employees will accept you as you are, no doubt less than perfect but doing your best. The one behavior that talented people seldom tolerate for long is disrespect. If you wish to keep them, it is absolutely critical that you recognize each person's unique qualities and then demonstrate your respect in consistent, undeniable ways.

Alas

We lost one of our most important paralegal assistants. Every attorney in our office counted on her, and we were shocked to see her go. In her exit interview, she said it was not the pay or perks that caused her to seek a new job. It was the daily and weekly indignities that she suffered while trying to do her best in this job. Her performance review (and possible raise) had been overlooked for the past six months. Her request to join an association of paralegals still lay on her boss's desk after six weeks. She was denied attendance at a free seminar that would have benefited the firm, because they couldn't free her up. She had not been thanked for her hard work and excellent results. Her boss grunted and vented and took out his frustrations on her without giving it a second thought. She finally left the firm because she did not feel respected or valued, but she did feel used and demeaned. And everyone noticed.

—Attorney, major law firm

Could that happen at your workplace? Have you, or has someone you know (even one of your direct reports), ever left for reasons like that?

Different Strokes

You cannot respect and honor others unless you respect—even celebrate—the differences between people. Can you imagine how ineffective (and boring) your team would be if everyone thought the same, looked the same, believed the same, had the same talents? Most of us readily accept the notion that diversity of talent and perspective strengthens a work group and contributes to excellent results. Yet if we are honest, we admit that differences also get in the way. The hard truth is that many of us more often tolerate than celebrate differences.

The Museum of Tolerance in Los Angeles welcomes its visitors in a unique way. As a tour group forms in the lobby, they are invited into a waiting room that admits them into the museum. Our tour guide said to us, "Notice that there are two doors through which you may enter this museum. One is marked 'prejudiced' and the other is marked 'unprejudiced.' You may enter through whichever door represents you." There was a long pause as people pondered what they should do, which door to choose. Finally a man bravely stepped forward and turned the knob on the door marked "unprejudiced." A few stepped forward to follow him, while the rest of us watched. He turned the knob, looked a little confused and then turned red with embarrassment as he realized the door was locked. We could only enter the museum through the door marked "prejudiced."

—Sharon Jordan-Evans

Which door would you have chosen? What would your reaction be to the locked door? It is important for most of us to take a good look at our preferences and prejudices, our *leanings*. We all have them. They pop up when we mentor and coach, promote, reward, punish, and hire (research shows we are most apt to hire someone like ourselves). Once you take note of your leanings, you can begin to see the impact they might have on your employees.

Museum of Tolerance designers assumed that we all carry prejudices. The issue is how we respond. The first step in leveraging differences is to take a good look at your own beliefs. How much do you respect people who are very different from yourself? Do you value what they bring to your team? How badly do you want them to stay?

TO DO . . .

✓ Analyze your attitudes and prejudices. Admit to your leanings toward or away from those with different

- Skin color
- Status
- Personality
- Age

- Education
- Height or weight
- Title
- Accent
- Geographic origin
- Job function
- Gender
- Lifestyle
- Sexual orientation
- Talent
- _____ (add one)
- _____ (add another)

✓ Add to the list above. What do you tend to lean toward or away from?

✓ Notice how your *leanings* play out at work. Whom did you last promote? Whom do you tend to ignore, praise less often, and be less friendly with?

✓ Learn about the differences among your employees. One manager held a discovery day, where people were encouraged to talk about themselves, how they grew up, the holidays they observe, and why.

✓ Leverage the differences. Roosevelt Thomas, a diversity consultant and author, defines diversity as "the maximum utilization of talent in the workforce."[13] Appreciate and utilize individual strengths, styles, and talents.

✓ *Decide* to change. Practice fairness, and consciously avoid discriminating in the old familiar ways. Your employees will notice.

Sometimes conveniences, traditions, and preferences disguise themselves as requirements.

—Anonymous

When people get their backs up about diversity, often they're resisting what they see as an effort to change how they feel. Valuing differences does not force you to change how you feel. It's about how you act at work to keep good employees.

Remember that there is no genetic predisposition to bias, no bias gene rides on your chromosomes; no DNA test can identify who is biased and who is not. Bias is learned. It's an acquired habit of thought rooted in fear and fueled by conditioning and, as such, can be unacquired and deconditioned. That's good news because no one can afford to allow his or her distorted vision interfere with the ability to function effectively, fairly, and successfully in increasingly diverse workplaces.

—Sondra Thiederman

Sloppy Moods

Honoring others and treating them with dignity and respect may mean managing your moods. Have you ever worked for someone with roller-coaster moods? You know, one day he's up; the next he's *way* down. While it is human to have ups and downs, it is grownup to manage those moods so that they do not hurt others. Some call moods that have run amok *sloppy moods.* They are simply uncontrolled. Whatever is felt comes spilling out and slops all over employees (or family). The results can be embarrassment, hurt, anger, humiliation, and loss of dignity.

see JERK

TO DO ...

✓ If you are guilty of sloppy moods, take notice and take control. Get away from others while you work through your difficulties. Go to your room; take a *time-out.*

✓ If you happen to slop on someone, apologize. To err is human, and most people appreciate an apology; it is a sign of respect.

✓ If you have a serious problem managing your moods, consider seeking help from a professional or your organization's Employee Assistance Program (EAP).

Are They Invisible?

My previous boss never said hello to me. He would walk right past me in the hall as if I did not exist, or was invisible. He did say hello to every vice president. My new boss treats me with respect. I feel like she values me as a person, even though her job level is above mine. I love working here.

—Bank teller

When employees talk about the disrespect that drove them out the door to a new job, they sometimes refer to this feeling of invisibility. You might be simply lost in thought when you pass your employees in the hall and fail to acknowledge them. But they will notice and may feel less than honored or respected.

TO DO . . .

✓ Notice your employees. Pay attention as you walk down the halls and say hello to them by name.

✓ Smile, shake hands, greet your employees, and introduce them to others, even those of higher rank. They will feel honored and definitely not invisible.

Trust Me

Some say that trust is a gift. Others say it must be earned. Still others refuse to trust anyone at all. Andy Grove, chairman of Intel, even wrote a book called *Only the Paranoid Survive*. Great title, but in practice it is a tough way to live!

What we know is that when you trust your employees, most will be trustworthy. They will feel honored and respected when you trust them with important tasks and heavy responsibilities and when you let them do things their way. When you fail to trust them, they will often feel dishonored, disrespected, and undervalued. And you can bet they will leave when a better opportunity presents itself.

If you doubt this, think about a time in your career when you had a boss who trusted you implicitly, trusted you to excel, trusted you with information or assets. How did you feel? What was your level of commitment to the boss or the organization as a result?

Alas

He simply could not learn to trust us. It was as if he thought we were all out to get him, and in the end it was almost a self-fulfilling prophecy. We knew we were worthy of his trust, and yet we almost began to feel guilty as he micromanaged us and constantly looked over our shoulders. We had to account for every minute of our time and every nickel we spent. Finally it was just too demeaning. The entire team decided to find other employment and a boss who trusted us.

—Director, engineering firm

If only the boss had trusted his team. They were truly not out to get him—they were just trying to do their jobs. To trust someone implicitly shows tremendous respect for that person.

Nine out of ten employees say that true success is about being trusted to get the job done.[14]

TO DO . . .

✓ Check out your own ability to trust others. Do you tend to offer trust as a gift or demand evidence of trustworthiness before you give it?

✓ Try trusting your employees. Say you trust them, act like you trust them, and *really* trust them. Give them responsibility and then let them carry it out.

What's Fair Is Fair

Talented workers will leave a boss who is perceived to be unfair. Unfair treatment translates to disrespect in many employees' minds. Check out your communication approach and your actions with your employees. How do they view the decisions and changes that you make? What seems fair or unfair to them? Do you honor their ideas, and do you care about their reactions? If you don't, you will lose them.

> *Always do what is right. It will gratify most of the people, and astound the rest.*
>
> —Mark Twain

Anybody Home?

Sometimes busy bosses seem almost unreachable. Unless the sky is falling (by their definition), it is virtually impossible to get their attention. An employee wants to leave early on Friday for his son's baseball game and asks you on the Monday before. Another employee needs your okay to attend a conference in two months. A third employee's wife has been hospitalized with a life-threatening illness. What do you do? Ideally you respond quickly in all three cases.

Unfortunately, too many busy bosses tell the first and second employees that they will get back to them but never do. The employees feel unimportant and disrespected and have to either nag for an answer or forget the whole thing (but they never really do). And what does the busy boss do about the third employee? Too often, nothing. Treating an employee with dignity means acknowledging how difficult and unique this life situation is.

My mother was dying of cancer and lived 1,000 miles away. I was a wreck at work, unable to concentrate, and feeling so guilty about not being with her. My boss took me into his office and told me to take as much time as I needed to go and be with my mother in her final days. I will never forget that act. I felt so valued and respected by him that my commitment to the organization soared.

—Secretary, consulting firm

TO DO . . .

✓ Listen to your employees' wants and needs. Even concerns that seem small or insignificant are clearly important to them.
✓ Respond to their requests quickly. Don't wait for them to nag you.
✓ Be aware and take steps to help employees in their times of need. They will pay you back a thousandfold.

BOTTOM LINE

Respecting others may seem easy enough. After all, it's really just an attitude, isn't it? Attitudes and beliefs are at the core of showing respect and honoring others. But behaviors and actions are involved, too. Check out your beliefs about differences, and audit your actions. Listen to your employees, respond to them, and—bottom line—treat them with respect and dignity.

Chapter 5

ENRICH

Energize the Job

The job just became ho-hum. I mean, I was good at it, my customers were pleased, but I was just plain bored.

—A.J.

Did your own "job EKG" ever go flat? Did the feeling of challenge change to a feeling of routine? Did you think something was missing? What happened to your energy? In any case, did you start to wonder what else there was? Did you start to look around?

It Can Happen to Anyone

Unfortunately, your most valued employees are the most likely to suffer this sense of job discontent. By definition, they are savvy, creative, self-propelled, and energetic. They need stimulating work, opportunities for personal challenge and growth, and a contributing stake in the organizational action. If good workers find the job with your company no longer provides these necessities, they may decide they have outgrown the place and will consider leaving.

Some employees, perhaps not the obvious stars, but people with solid potential, suffer discontent yet stay on the job. Instead of leaving for the next challenge, they find ways to disengage. Their departure is psycho-

42

logical rather than physical. It shows up in counterproductive activities like absenteeism and mediocre performance. These individuals simply withhold their energy and effort, figuring, "What's the point anyway?"

Either way, departure or disengagement, you lose talented people who are vital to the success of your unit and your company—a preventable loss. Employees who depart or disengage because they are not content in their current jobs are telling you that *something is lacking in the work itself.* The job may provide good pay, enjoyable and respected coworkers, adequate security, and appropriate benefits. It may be with an excellent company doing important work. However, the day-to-day elements of getting the work done may not provide the stimulation, growth, future possibilities, or current sense of achievement that make an employee want to stay and to contribute wholeheartedly.

Alas

I had been doing the same work for seven years when my organization decided to expand the business in a new direction. I met with my boss to tell him that I would love to learn about the new side of the business and maybe expand my job to include at least some work in the new arena. I wasn't sure how it could all fit, but I knew I wanted something new and exciting in my day-to-day work life. When I raised the topic, he responded curtly, "The team has already been chosen to do this new work. We need you to keep doing what you're doing." That was the end of our discussion. I left the organization six months later.

—Claims adjuster, insurance company

Get Enriched Quick

Job enrichment means structuring ways for employees to get the growth, challenge, and renewal they seek without leaving their current jobs or organizations.

Change in what your employees do (content) or how they do it (process) is the key. Job enrichment allows employees to take on different tasks and responsibilities or to accomplish them in ways that promote personal autonomy and creativity.

An enriched job does the following:

✓ Gives employees room to initiate, create, and implement new ideas
✓ Promotes setting and achieving personal and group goals
✓ Allows employees to see their contributions to an end product or goal
✓ Challenges employees to expand their knowledge and capabilities
✓ Has a future beyond itself

A job can be as neatly tailored to a worker's peculiar goals and requirements as a pair of Levi's [jeans] to an online customer's imperfect physique.

—David Ulrich and David Sturm

If enrichment is so beneficial, why isn't it a standard part of every job? One good reason is this: What enriches one employee is different from what enriches the next. Courtney, devastated by her job's predictability, craves variety in each day's tasks. Marco, tired of being told how to do his audit reports, is ready to teach someone else how to do them. Lindsey sees that her computer programs meet the needs of her superiors and now wants to know how her programs are used by the company. How do you tailor job enrichment to individuals and their needs? Ask them.

see ASK

TO DO . . .

Try the following questions to help people probe their work lives for possibilities of enrichment:

✓ Do you know how your job is important to the company?
✓ What skills do you use on the job? What talents do you have that you don't use?
✓ What about your job do you find challenging? Rewarding?

✓ In what areas would you like increased responsibility for your current tasks?
✓ What would you like to be doing in the next three to five years?
✓ In what ways would you like your job changed?

The idea is to help your people evaluate their jobs and discover ideas for enrichment. These ideas will, and should, vary greatly among employees. Be prepared for requests and discussions that center on these points:

✓ Greater autonomy: opportunities for self-direction, responsibility for independence, and discretion in determining work procedures
✓ Increased feedback from clients, coworkers, and you
✓ Participation in decisions about work processes before they are cast in stone
✓ Opportunities for teamwork with people from other departments as well as their own
✓ Increased variety in tasks
✓ More opportunities to affect the organization or colleagues' work
✓ Contact with clients to learn about their problems and perspectives
✓ New challenges and learning beyond current levels

Remember, this is an important discussion and doesn't have to be handled in one conversation. Don't feel as if you have to have all the answers, and don't let yourself become the "fix-it" person. These discussions should be collaborative. Both of you need to do the creative thinking that is necessary to bring back the "juice" of the job.

The Learning Assignment: A Key Enrichment Challenge

What if you don't train them—and they stay?

—Anonymous

Many people feel that their jobs are getting better when they can learn or improve a skill. Once you identify a skill, turn one of these three levels of learning into assignments that grow someone on the job:

LEVEL 1. Conscious Observation. Select an expert for an employee to observe—someone who does the particular skill exceptionally well. After the observation period, discuss what your employee noticed, learned, or thinks could be done differently (for example, watch someone who is a superb negotiator).

LEVEL 2. Selected Participation. Give the employee a chance to take a well-defined but limited role using a new skill. Make sure the employee has the opportunity to get his or her feet wet without feeling overwhelmed (for example, prepare the opening remarks in the negotiation with the vendor). Again, providing feedback is essential.

LEVEL 3. Key Responsibility. Give an employee primary responsibility for a project that requires full use of a new skill or competency. Choose a project that provides visibility and accountability. (For example, complete the entire negotiation with the vendor.) Provide feedback at the end of the assignment, or ask someone skilled in this area to do it. Step in only if necessary.

It's in Your Control

By now you might be shaking your head and saying, "Oh great, they all want fascinating work and more money." Slow down. Plenty of job enrichment possibilities are in your control. Here are some techniques that have worked:

A Checklist of Enrichment Possibilities

see OPPORTUNITIES

✓ *Combine tasks.* The auto industry discovered long ago that an employee doing a single, small repetitive task—painting the trim around the wheel wells—will not be as challenged and motivated as an employee involved in a related set of tasks, such as painting and stripping an entire car.

✓ *Form teams.* Self-directed work groups can make a lot of their own decisions. They can redistribute work, so that team members learn more, have more variety, and follow more projects through to completion.

✓ ***Put employees in touch with clients.*** For example, a computer systems troubleshooter might be more effective knowing the needs of real people and units rather than responding only to problems as they occur. Assign one troubleshooter to one department, and make her accountable for the computer system. Give her a client. Clients can be inside or outside the organization. It's amazing how many employees never see them.

✓ ***Rotate assignments.*** New responsibilities can help an employee feel challenged and valued. Employees can acquire important new skills that add depth to the workforce. Do rotational assignments sound like chaos? Suggest the idea and let your employees propose the "who" and "how" part; you'll be surprised at their expertise in making it happen smoothly.

✓ ***Build in feedback.*** Do more than annual reviews. Find ways to develop peer review and client review opportunities. Employees want to know about their performance, and continual feedback allows them to be their own quality-control agents.

✓ ***Establish widespread participation.*** Employees are empowered and motivated when they take part in decisions that have an impact on their work, such as budget and hiring decisions, or ways to organize work and schedules. Involvement allows employees to see the big picture and enables them to make a contribution they find meaningful.

✓ ***Nurture creativity.*** Untapped creativity dwindles. If employees rarely think for themselves, they lose the ability to contribute their best ideas. They simply go through the paces, undermotivated and disengaged. You can help by asking for and rewarding creative ideas, by giving employees the freedom and resources to create, and by challenging employees with new assignments, tasks, and learning.

We weren't thrilled when our boss first said we might be "going digital." But then he let us check out the system ourselves and implement it in our own way and our own time frame. I set up a special test with one of the doctors to see how it would work. We had to get creative and revise some work processes. It actually turned out to be fun, and we found a more efficient way to get the work done.

—Medical transcriptionist

✓ ***Set goals.*** Ideally, each employee should set enrichment goals. You can help by asking individuals and teams for those goals each year. Be sure they make sense to the individual, the work group, and the organization.

TO DO . . .

Test the motivating potential of an enrichment goal by asking your employee any or all of these questions:

✓ What's in it for you?
- How will it increase your marketability in your profession?
- How will it increase your reputation as a specialist or generalist?
- How will it help you gain more confidence and competence in your current position?

✓ What's in it for your work group?
- How will it help you work more effectively with your current team?
- How will it increase/enhance your contribution to your work group or department?
- How does it build new collaborations or extend your network?

✓ What's in it for the organization?
- How will it increase your value to the organization?
- How does it contribute to current organizational mission, strategy, or goals?
- How does it address a current relevant business need?

BOTTOM LINE

Workplace boredom is a major cause of turnover. If you fail to take steps to discover when your talented employees' jobs have become routine, you run the risk of losing them, physically or psychologically. Job enrichment is not tricky or difficult. But it does require staying alert to opportunities for all your employees and encouraging them to suggest ways to enrich their own jobs.

Chapter 6

FAMILY

Get Friendly

Now this wasn't a big thing, but it certainly added to everything else. There was one time that I remember distinctly, when my child was in a soccer game and I wanted to attend. My manager made it clear that he did not approve of my leaving work early to see her game.

—A.J.

How are things at home? How are your folks? When was the last time you had a special lunch with a family member who needs more time with you? Is anyone at home complaining about not seeing enough of you?

What good is a high-powered career if it makes you miserable?
What good is owning a beautiful house if you're never home?
What good is being passionate about a hobby if you never have the free time to pursue it? [15]

People quit when rigid workplace rules cause unbearable family stress. Would they leave your organization over work/family conflicts? Yes. Business magazines have spent plenty of ink in recent years on the importance of developing a "family-friendly culture." But what does it really mean?

Employees are asking for a workplace that helps them balance the demands of their work and family lives, rather than forcing them to choose one over the other. Today and from now on, organizations that are not family-friendly will definitely have a harder time getting their good people to stay.

Talented employees do not have to look far to find family-friendly employers who offer features like these:

✓ Childcare facilities or subsidies
✓ Flexible work schedules
✓ Job sharing
✓ Telecommuting
✓ Eldercare assistance (such as referral programs)
✓ Extended and creative maternity or paternity leave programs

These savvy employers give talented employees flexibility in how they work, when they work, and often where they work. They allow employees to meet personal responsibilities while still being productive at work.

If your organization does have these policies and perks in place, that's great. But if not, you have two options. One is to benchmark. Get smart about what other organizations are offering, and then go to your manager (and/or the human resources department) with information and suggestions. See if you can get some of these ideas adopted in your organization. Whether or not you take the first option, you can take the more urgent one: become a more family-friendly manager. There are things that you can do to support your employees' lives outside of work. The result will be more dedicated workers who are less likely to stray. We recommend that you pursue both options.

What Does Family Mean, and What Do They Want?

What do we mean by the word *family*? Some of you might immediately picture small children and a mom and dad. Others picture a young newlywed couple, a Gen-X-er and his dog, or a single male caring for his aging father. (Fourteen million U.S. workers care for aging family members and report higher levels of stress than workers with dependents or children.[16])

> *A letter to the editor in* Inc. *magazine said, "I read with great interest the article about the benefits of on-site daycare. Inc could follow that up with an article titled, "Can I Bring the Folks?" Everything that holds true for child care holds true for eldercare. Adult children having to look after their elderly relatives will be the next care crisis for employees.*
>
> —Bruce Hurwitz, Ph.D.

> *A survey of U.S. companies by MetLife . . . indicated a $29 billion loss of productivity because of employee turnover, missed days, and reduced workloads relating to elder care. By 2020, 53 million Americans will be 65 and older. Demands on their adult children will continue to rise. The time to prepare is now.*
>
> —Inc., August 2004

see ASK

One family-friendly strategy won't meet all of these employees' individual needs. It's critical to consider the different types of families in your group, and then think about (and talk about) the approaches that will work best for each of them. Remember, the most accurate way to get this information quickly is simply to ask your employees.

TO DO . . .

✓ Ask your employees questions like this: "What would make your life easier?" In their answers, look for small things that you, their manager, might be able to do to help. Brainstorm with your employees to create some innovative solutions to their work/family challenges.

Get Flexible

You may feel restricted by your organization's lack of family-friendly programs or policies. Yet you have tremendous opportunities to get *family-friendly* within your own work group. What you do (and fail to do) as a manager can mean so much to your employees as they juggle work and family. And much of what you can do as a manager costs you and your organization little or nothing.

Alas

Ernie was frustrated and exhausted trying to manage his work and family life. His wife also worked, and they had a six-month-old baby. Ernie wanted to partner with his wife in raising their child, so he began to flex his hours a bit to pick up the baby at childcare or take her to the doctor. His productivity and work quality remained high, but his hours dropped (from 55 to 45 a week) and looked somewhat erratic. The boss told Ernie that he simply had to return to his previous schedule—end of discussion. Even though Ernie tried to explain his needs, the boss had no time and no tolerance. Within two months Ernie had found a new job, one with a family-friendly culture and a boss who allowed him flexibility in his schedule.

Ernie's boss lost a valuable employee, one who may be very costly to replace, because he did not take the time to listen and to design a family-friendly work solution with his employee. Rigidity cost him dearly. Think flexibly the next time an employee asks you for different work hours or time off to help a spouse, parent, or friend. Think about the real costs of saying yes. Will productivity suffer? Will you set a dangerous precedent? Will that employee begin to take advantage of you? It is more likely that your employees will applaud (maybe silently) your open-mindedness and willingness to help a valued employee in a time of need. Remember to set clear expectations for your employees' results and hold them to those results. Then you will have room to flex when it matters.

Get Supportive

Some managers mistakenly think that they should clearly separate themselves from their employees' personal lives. You have much more to gain by showing your interest in their lives outside of work.

I was so excited about my daughter's singing debut at her high school. She had been taking vocal lessons, she had developed a strong, beautiful voice, and that day was her chance to show it off. She would sing the "Star Spangled Banner" (without accompaniment) during the all-school pep rally at 1 P.M. My boss was excited for me and said, "No problem," when I asked him if I could go watch her. But here's the best part. When I returned, with videotape in hand, he asked me how it went and asked if I would show him the tape. It was such a small thing but meant so much to me. I proudly showed him the video and beamed as he praised my daughter. He showed support in so many ways that day.

—Receptionist, manufacturing firm

We have heard about managers who became involved in several appropriate ways. As you read these approaches, think about which ones might work for you and your employees:

✓ Allowing employees' children to come to work with them occasionally, usually to celebrate a special occasion or because of a special need.

✓ Driving to an employee's house to be with her and her family following a death in the family.

✓ Accompanying employees to their children's ball games and recitals.

✓ Inviting an employee and his or her parents, relatives, or children to lunch.

✓ Allowing well-behaved pets into the workplace. (Believe it or not, there's a Web site, www.dogfriendly.com, dedicated to pet-friendly workplaces.)

✓ Staying late after work to help employees work on Halloween costumes for their children.

✓ Researching eldercare alternatives for an employee who needs help with aging parents.

✓ Sending birthday cards or cakes to employees' family members.

✓ Setting up special e-mail and resource areas on the company intranet for employees' children.

✓ Locating resources (the company lawyer) for an employee struggling with the health insurance company.

Here is an example of really showing support:

When people ask me why I stayed at my company for 27 years, I tell them this story: When I was pregnant with my first child—he's now 24—I had trouble with my pregnancy and was sent home for bed rest. After two weeks, I couldn't take it anymore and went back to work. The president of the company called me and said, "I am not going to allow you to go back and forth on the subway." He just sent his car in the morning and took me home at night. At that time, I became a lifetime employee of that organization.

—Chairman and CEO, advertising agency

Get Creative

"We've never done that here." "The policies don't support that." "I'd be in hot water with my boss if I allowed that." These are common excuses among managers who don't know their real power or are afraid to test the limits of the family-friendly (or unfriendly) rules. Sure, there are constraints and policy guidelines in most organizations. And you have to play by those rules to some degree. But often it pays to get creative on behalf of your employees and their needs.

see QUESTION

There was no such thing as job sharing in this organization. We have a long history and cemented policies. After the birth of our children, another director and I decided to go to our boss and ask about the possibility of sharing one job. The job was high level and critical to the organization, so at first there was tremendous concern about even trying it. But our boss took a risk and gained approval for a six-month test period. That was 12 years ago and we have been sharing the job effectively ever since. The creativity and flexibility of our boss allowed us both to balance family and work. We are tremendously grateful and loyal employees.

—Manager, public utility

Job sharing is just one example of a creative solution to a challenging situation. Here are some other strategies and solutions that managers have come up with in collaboration with their employees. Which might work for you?

✓ If employees must travel on weekends, offer something in exchange, such as comp time during the week or allowing family members to travel with the employee.

✓ When your employees travel to areas where they have family or friends, allow them to spend extra time with those people at the beginning or end of the trip.

✓ If company policy absolutely prohibits bringing pets to work, consider a picnic in a park where those furry family members are welcome.

✓ Give your employees a "floating" day off per year to be used for a special occasion. Or suggest they go home early on their birthdays or anniversaries.

✓ Have a party for your team and their families. Invite the kids (or hire sitters for small ones), and go for pizza together.

✓ When an employee asks about working from home, really explore that possibility. What are the upsides? Downsides? Get creative about how that might work to benefit both the employee and your team.

TO DO . . .

✓ Do your employees already have computers at home? Consider subsidizing the Internet costs so that they can work from home on an as-needed basis. The monthly costs for Internet use are small compared to the productivity you'll get in return.

The best kind of creativity is collaborative. Remember to brainstorm a list of ideas *with your employees* and be continuously open to new and innovative ways to balance family and work. Tailor and customize your strategies to employees' needs.

BOTTOM LINE

Good employees leave family-unfriendly workplaces.

Do some of these ideas seem extreme to you? We suggest talking to your company's recruiter about the options some employers are including in recruitment packages. If your definition of family-friendly is allowing your employees to accept an occasional personal phone call, it's time to find out what's going on around you. There are positive pay-offs for your efforts, including increased loyalty, money saved, and the competitive edge that a loyal and committed workforce will provide. Become a family-friendly manager and keep your talent on your team.

Chapter 7

GOALS

Expand Options

The only career path I saw was up—and up was in short supply.

—A.J.

Do you get a knot in your stomach when a valued employee begins a conversation with one of these phrases?

✓ I'd like to talk to you about my career.
✓ I really want to understand what my career options are.
✓ I'm interested in talking about my next step.
✓ I don't understand why he got that promotion. I thought I . . . .
✓ It's only through a step up that I feel appreciated.

Feel the knot? It's understandable. You value employees with superb skills who have mastered the current job and want more. They may get calls from recruiters. They want a chance to run the project. They're in your office, looking to you for a much-needed, much-deserved conversation about moving up in the organization. You want to keep them. And "up" is in short supply.

You may lose some of them. However, our 20 years of research reveal that not all those who say they want vertical moves will leave if they don't get them. But they *will* leave (physically or psychologically) if they are not challenged, growing, and having new experiences.

Moving Forward Instead of Up

What if your employees began to think about other ways of moving? What if each move challenged and rewarded them? What if they could move forward instead of up?

Sometimes you can prevent turnover by helping your employees identify several career goals. If employees see that you can support several viable alternatives, they will picture a future for themselves within your organization.

Right Person, Right Place, Right Time

The above phrase is the goal that human resource professionals and managers target. It's never been easy to achieve. But here's a twist to consider: What if there were more *right* places? Would there not be more *right* times for all those *right* people?

We believe that there are five possible moves in addition to moving up. We also believe that the more specifically you can outline those moves, the less likely your talented employees will see *other* grass as greener. Consider talking with your employees about moves in several (or all) of the following directions:

1. Lateral movement: Moving across or horizontally
2. Enrichment: Growing in place
3. Exploration: Temporary moves intended for researching other options
4. Realignment: Moving downward to open new opportunities
5. Relocation: Moving to another organization

If you notice that four of these options (all but enrichment) raise the possibility of your talented people moving away from you, you're right.

see CAREER

If this makes you nervous, you're in the majority. If you've built a strong, functioning team, you don't want to lose key talent to other managers and other parts of the organization. Some managers are so fearful that they hoard their talent, failing to expose them to other opportunities. Ironically, that strategy backfires and some of the best people walk— often to the competitor.

So why should you help your best people expand their options, even if it means they leave your team? Here are some possibilities:

✓ People love to work for someone who cares enough to help them with their careers. They'll actually stay a little longer with a development-minded manager.

✓ Your efforts could save talent for the enterprise and keep them from the competition.

✓ You will gain a reputation as a manager who cares about people and their development. That reputation will draw other talented people your way.

✓ You may gain personal satisfaction from helping others develop.

One of the authors once worked for a large corporation where she and her manager had a great relationship for many years. One day an opportunity surfaced that clearly would make even better use of her skills. Her manager, she later learned, lost a lot of sleep over this. Losing the employee meant losing a valuable asset to the team, but encouraging her move to a new start-up division would be a win for the employee and the organization. The manager bit the bullet, and a phenomenal opportunity resulted. The employee stayed with the organization for several productive years, and her manager enjoyed a reputation as a strong people-developer.

Lateral Movement

Until recently, lateral moves meant that your career might be headed for a dead end. Not today. Lateral moves offer much-needed breadth of experience. Taking a lateral move should mean applying current experience in a new job at the same level, but with different duties or challenges. Help employees see that lateral moves can improve skills or shift them from a slow-growing function to an expanding part of the organization. As you hold this discussion, be sure your people understand that you're not trying to get rid of them but to retain their talent for the organization.

TO DO . . .

Ask your employees

✓ Which of your skills can be applied beyond your present job and present department?
✓ If you make a lateral move, what long-term career opportunities does it provide?
✓ What three skills are most transferable to another department?
✓ What other department interests you?

Enrichment

This might be the easiest option to discuss—but it's also one of the most ignored. Most folks seem to think they need to move out of their current position to develop. Never has this been less true. Most of your employees' work is changing constantly. Enrichment means that employees expand the job, refine their expertise, or find depth in areas they really enjoy. You can help.

Here's the critical question for you (and them) to ponder: What can employees do, or learn to do, that will energize their work and bring them closer to achieving their goals and the goals of the organization?

see ENRICH

I worked for a great boss as a project manager, but I knew (and she really knew, too) that I could do more. I had fantastic artistic skills (if I do say so myself), and my boss did something about it. She sent me to graphic recording school and has used my new skills in her business. I am thrilled!

—Project manager

TO DO . . .

Try asking your employees these questions:

✓ What do you enjoy most about your job?
✓ What could be added to your job to make it more satisfying?
✓ What assignment would advance you further in your current work?
✓ Which of your current tasks is the most routine?

Exploration

It happens. We reach a stage in our careers when we aren't sure of what we want or what choices are available, or even what's appropriate. We need information to decide if the grass is indeed greener elsewhere. Encourage your people to consider options like these:

✓ Taking short-term job assignments in other parts of the organization
✓ Participating on project teams with people from other departments
✓ Scheduling informational interviews (These are interviews with people whose job your employee *thinks* he or she wants.)

see OPPORTUNITIES

Giving a talented person whose expertise you need the chance to explore other teams isn't easy. But people are less likely to feel trapped in their current jobs when they have other choices. They may find out that the grass isn't greener.

TO DO . . .

Consider asking your employees the following questions:

✓ What other areas of the company interest you?

✓ If you could start your career over, what would you do differently?

✓ Which of our current organization task forces interest you? Which might give you the best view of another part of this organization?

✓ Whose job would you like to learn more about?

Realignment

In the old world of "up is the only way," the thought of moving downward would probably be last on anyone's list of options. But sometimes the path to a career goal involves a step backward to gain a better position for the next move.

Alas

An excellent technical contributor was promoted to manager. At first he liked the work. It still had some technical components, and he managed other bright individual contributors. But over time he moved more and more into managing those bright others, searching for ways to bring more work to the unit, and fighting administrative battles. He felt he had made a mistake and longed to return to a technical position. He had outgrown his previous position but longed for something with the new hardware group. He went to his manager to admit his mistake and request a move. His manager resisted, suggesting he give it more time or that he enroll in a training course to improve his management skills. Instead, he applied for and got a job that was precisely what he wanted, with a competitor.

This company lost a talented person because neither he nor his manager discussed realignment.

TO DO . . .

Try one of these with an employee:

✓ If you take an assignment in another area, what will be the new opportunities for growth and development?
✓ Are you willing to accept the same or a lower salary to make a fresh start in a new area?
✓ How could a realigned position enable you to use the skills you really enjoy?
✓ Do you miss the technical, hands-on work you used to do?

Relocation

Why even mention relocation when we're talking about retention? Why don't we suggest that it means a move to another group within your own organization? The answer is, because it doesn't. Relocation means that you've thought about all the options, and you realize that the best career step for this employee is to look elsewhere. This might happen when one of the following scenarios applies:

✓ An employee's skills, interests, and values just don't fit his or her work
✓ An employee's career goals are unrealistic for your organization
✓ An employee is committed to pursuing entrepreneurial interests
✓ An employee's technical skills are undervalued in the organization

So how is relocation a retention vehicle? Most employees who have had this kind of straight talk conversation with their own managers do move on. Often they end up being the best ambassadors for that organization after they leave!

Don't have the relocation conversation unless you and your employee have really searched your *internal* labor market.

TO DO...

Consider asking these questions:

✓ Do you know people who have left this company and have gone somewhere else? What were their experiences like? Can you talk with these individuals before deciding what to do?
✓ What is it about this company that's making you want to look outside? How has the company changed?
✓ If you leave here, what are your long-term career opportunities in another organization?

When Up *Is* the Only Way

Sometimes, it's the only choice. Yes, vertical advancement up the corporate ladder is the classic move. Your job is to identify and communicate what a talented employee's vertical options could include. Of course, advancement is most likely when an employee's abilities match the needs of the organization. You must interpret the organization's strategic direction to your team so that they select assignments that will prepare them for coming changes and openings. Clearly, technical excellence and political savvy are both critical to gaining that next step. Talented people need straight feedback and continual coaching to reach their vertical career goals.

TO DO...

Try asking your employees the following:

✓ Who is your competition for that next position? What are his or her strengths and weaknesses?

✓ How has your job performance been during the last year? How has it prepared you for the next step?

✓ Why should this company promote you?

✓ What are the satisfactions and headaches that might come with this vertical move?

The More Choices, the Better

Consider . . .	If your employee . . .
Lateral	Wants to gain experience or skills in new areas
	Wants to use skills in a faster growth area or with new people
Enrichment	Wants to accomplish a better job fit
	Wants a change in pace
	Wants to use new skills or put old skills back to work
Vertical	Wants more responsibility and authority
Exploration	Isn't sure what else to do or where else to go
Realignment	Wants to relieve job stress
	Wants to move back to a technical job from management
	Wants to move to a new career path
Relocation	Can't find a good job fit

SORT for Reality

Once you have had discussions about options, it is important that you talk about whether the goal is realistic. Unrealistic goals cause many to lose face and faith, making outside options more attractive.

To Test If Goals Are . . .	Ask Employees . . .
Specific	Do others understand your goal the same way you do?
	How do you know?
	Can you clarify it further?
	Have you specified the type of job, organization, or function?
	Can you describe the goal in more detail?

To Test If Goals Are . . .	Ask Employees . . .
Obtainable	How do you see this as a logical next step for you?
	How likely is there to be a need in that area?
	What kind of competition can you expect?
	Do you have the necessary qualifications? Are there steps you can take to become more qualified?
Realistic	How is this goal consistent with your present position, skills, and abilities?
	How does this goal support your current values and future interests?
	How is this goal consistent with the organizational climate?
	How does this goal support the organization's future needs and policies?
Time-Bound	How realistic is the time frame
	• Given how frequently openings occur?
	• Given how long it will take to develop the required skills?
	• Given the length of time on the current job?
	• Given the anticipated needs of the organization?

BOTTOM LINE

Helping employees reach their goals often means helping them consider moves they may not have taken seriously before. Ask key questions to help them see what they could gain by trying a move that isn't a simple vertical step. You might surface choices they had not previously considered. The more options you can offer, the more you will increase your organization's chances of keeping the employee. And you will acquire a good reputation as a developer of people.

Chapter 8

IRE

Fit Is It

We hired in a hurry and didn't think about the fit between the new hires and the rest of the team. It ended up hurting everyone.

—A.J.

Get the right people in the door in the first place and you increase the odds of keeping them. As the manager, you have the clearest sense of the "right fit" for your department. Seems logical, doesn't it? Yet some managers see selection as a less important part of their jobs. They spend little time identifying the critical success factors for a position, preparing and conducting excellent interviews based on those factors, and, finally, evaluating and comparing the candidates before making a hiring decision. They may even delegate much of the hiring process to human resources instead of being involved themselves.

Hiring is, in fact, among the most important tasks you have as a manager, and you'll be doing a lot more of it, as Baby Boomers (the largest generation in the workforce) begin to leave the workplace and you search for their replacements. Hiring is a critical retention strategy. And it doesn't stop with the job offer. Today re-recruiting your best people is as critical as hiring them in the first place.

What Is Right Fit?

How do you know if a candidate will fit? How do you measure fit, manage your biases, and make more objective hiring decisions? Here is a start.

Measuring Fit

By "right fit" we mean a person whose skills and interests match the job requirements, and whose core values are consistent with the organization's values. Do your homework, be prepared, and be clear about your wants and needs.

> *Southwest Airlines looks for fit, especially with the company culture. A pilot told us about his own interview and selection process. He had heard that Southwest managers "hire for attitude and train for skill." The interviews they conducted with him certainly seemed to support that rumor. Through multiple interviews, he realized that the interviewers seemed to care more about who he was as a person than the fact that he had a stellar aviation background that should have made him an obvious choice. They probed for attitudes, beliefs, and behaviors that would give them clues about how he might treat flight attendants or peers, how he might deal with conflict at work, and what mattered most to him.*
>
> *Southwest managers tested his sense of humor in many ways during the series of interviews, and it became clear to him that they were truly looking for a fit between the way work gets done at Southwest Airlines and his personality.*

Why does Southwest care about an employee's sense of humor, especially the pilot's? Because Southwest's values include providing "outrageous customer service" and having *fun* at work. "Fit" also means alignment between the job requirements and the candidate's skills and interests. How often have you seen employees leave (on their own or with a push) because they simply did not have the right skills or interests?

Why didn't the hiring manager see the problem at the outset? How can you avoid that expensive mistake?

TO DO . . .

✓ *Analyze the job.* Get input from others to clarify the tasks, traits, and style required. Then create interview questions that will help you decide if the person has these skills or traits. (See the case study in the next section.)

✓ *Create an interview guide with your carefully crafted behavioral questions.* (Read on for some examples.) Behavioral questions allow you to learn how candidates have handled certain situations. Their answers will help you predict their ability to handle similar situations in the future. Use the same questions for all candidates so that you can make fair comparisons.

✓ *Include others in the interview process.* Have potential team members, direct reports, and peers of these future employees interview them (ideally asking different questions from yours) and give you their input. Several heads are definitely better than one when it comes to hiring.

✓ *Consider using personality and skill assessments to help you make the decision.* Get information from your human resources department about tools that might help you evaluate candidates' skills, work interests, and even values. Note: Don't rely on just one tool when making your decision.

In Search of Fit

Joe, a manager in a high-tech company, has an opening for a supervisor in the marketing department. He has placed Internet and newspaper ads and netted a stack of resumés to consider. With help from his human resources representative, he has narrowed the field to the top ten candidates. On paper, all ten have technical skills that are great fits for the job.

Joe is pretty savvy and has hired many people. Some worked out well, and some were absolute flops. All had looked good on paper. This time, though, Joe is prepared to get the *right fit!* He has identified the core values of his department. They include honesty, integrity, teamwork, customer focus, and work/life balance.

The critical leadership competencies for the role include motivating others, building a team, and dealing with ambiguity. Joe knows that the right fit will be a person with those skills. Next, Joe creates his interview guide with the questions he thinks can help him. Here are three questions on Joe's sheet:

see VALUES

1. Tell me about a work incident when you were totally honest, despite a potential risk or downside for the honesty.
2. How did you handle a recent situation where the direction from above was unclear and circumstances were changing?
3. Describe how you motivated a group of people to do something they did not want to do.

These questions may seem tough to answer, and they are. Joe allows time for the candidates to ponder the question and eases the tension by suggesting they take their time or by acknowledging it's a tough question. You can imagine that each of these questions leads Joe and his candidates into potentially deep discussions that could reveal where each candidate truly lines up on the value or leadership competency at hand. The questions are open-ended, so they can't be answered yes or no. They are not leading, as in, "Do you value work/life balance?" They are behavioral, forcing the candidates to cite real-life examples.

Joe takes notes so he will not forget some of their more critical answers or the assumptions he makes along the way. He probes to learn more about each topic until he feels he truly knows the candidates. Of course, he asks questions to validate their technical expertise.

Afterward, Joe compares notes with the other interviewers. He also looks at the assessment results to see if there are any red flags he should explore in follow-up interviews.

Joe compares his candidates by scoring them on a 1–5 scale (using 1 to indicate the absence of a skill and 5 to indicate a highly developed skill) on each of the critical success factors that he had identified for the job. They include

✓ Technical skills,
✓ Leadership competencies, and
✓ Values.

As he scores them, he reviews his notes and thinks about

✓ The level of each candidate's sincerity,
✓ Expressed enthusiasm and interest in the work, and
✓ Probable level of skill.

While there is no such thing as a totally objective interview or selection process, this method allows Joe to make the most objective decision possible. He proceeds to offer the job to the candidate whom he feels best meets the criteria.

By the way, had none of the candidates measured up to the criteria Joe set, he was willing to start over with a new batch of candidates. He had learned from past mistakes that it was too costly to settle for a mediocre hire.

Avoid Desperation Hiring

When candidates are few and your needs are immediate, you, too, can fall victim to the dangerous syndrome of *desperation hiring*. One manager, who claimed to have always done a terrific job of interviewing, analyzing, and selecting candidates, said he had narrowed his interview questions down to one: "When can you start?" Another said his favorite question was, "Can you fog a mirror?" (as in, "Are you breathing?").

If you're tempted to resort to desperation hiring, remember that today's hiring mistake is tomorrow's headache. You know how hard it is to rid your team of the wrong hire. (Someone recently suggested we write a sequel to *Love 'Em* called *How to Lose Your Losers*. Her point is well taken!)

A much sought-after new hire, when explaining how he chose which offer to select, said: "They put me first. They asked, 'What do you want to do?' 'What are your ideas?' and so on."

Be aware that talented candidates are well prepared and have many choices. Imagine that they arrive with a grid in their heads (or sometimes on paper). That grid might look like this:

My wants/needs (candidate)	Your organization	Your competitor	Another job
Compensation			
Perks			
Team			
Geography			
Training			
Creativity			
Vacation			
Opportunities to Advance			

This grid helps the candidate ask you questions, evaluate the opportunity somewhat objectively, and compare yours to other job opportunities.[17]

A survey of more than 800 MBAs from 11 leading North American and European schools found a substantial number were willing to forgo some financial benefits to work for an organization with a better reputation for corporate social responsibility and ethics.[18]

Be prepared to *sell* your organization or team to candidates by addressing the key issues they raise. Treat candidates more like customers than subordinates. Think carefully about what you and your team can offer, and be ready to give specific examples. For example, if you are offering a great team environment, demonstrate that by having all team members meet and briefly interview your top candidates. Think about your team or organizational "wow" factors—those things that differentiate you from the rest. Whatever your unique selling proposition, recognize it and leverage it during the interview. One manager in a training-focused organization said it well: "I can't offer you a job for life, but I can offer employability for life—here or somewhere."

Note: Remember—don't oversell. Painting a too-rosy picture can backfire when your new recruits find out that you were exaggerating.

> *A high-technology company recognized after several years of unsuccessful recruiting that it was simply not selling its organization. The recruiters and managers knew how terrific the culture was and that the technology was the best in the business. Once they began to spend more time in the interviews demonstrating their cutting-edge products, they began to grab the best of the best high-tech talent. They have now tripled the time they spend demonstrating products during key interviews.*

TO DO . . .

✓ Remember to sell talented prospects on your organization. Think about what makes your company unique and a great place to work.

✓ Listen carefully to what candidates are seeking. Be open to possibilities. Example: One company enticed its top choice by changing the job title from *Feed Salesman* to *Livestock Produce Specialist.*

✓ Place a copy of this book on your desk during the interview. (Candidates will get the hint that keeping good people is important to you.) To go a step further, show them the book and ask them which of the chapters (A–Z) are most relevant to retaining *them.*

Who, Me? Biased?

What if "right fit" means *like me* or *the right age* or *shape/size* or *gender* or *color?* It doesn't—or shouldn't. The "right fit" excuse has been used many times to put clones (usually clones of the boss) in jobs. That is certainly not what we mean by "right fit." In fact, if you spend the time to identify those critical factors that spell success for a particular job and then select people using those criteria, you are most apt to avoid dismissing potentially wonderful candidates.

We all have biases, and we often make assumptions based on them. Let's test some of your assumptions about getting the right person in the job. Ask yourself, as you read this list, "Have I ever thought this about a person or a job?" Be brutally honest—you don't have to tell anyone how you responded!

Assumption Testing

Assumption: Single mothers will be a risk because when their children are ill, they will not show up.

Fact: Some single moms so need this job that they will find a way to make it to work. Some have excellent contingency planning skills and have two or three backup plans when the kids are sick. (And remember—it is illegal to ask candidates if they are single moms or have children.)

Assumption: A seriously overweight person can't do this job because of the air travel required.

Fact: Overweight or obese individuals certainly can find ways of doing the job, even if it demands air travel. And remember, obesity is viewed by law as a disability and, therefore, is protected by the ADA (Americans with Disabilities Act). That means that you must consider accommodation for a candidate who is qualified to do the work.

Assumption: He is _____ (fill in the ethnicity) and therefore won't be the go-getter we need.

Fact: Ethnicity has no correlation to work traits or motivation.

Assumption: She has never done this exact job before, so she would be a huge hiring risk.

Fact: Although we often look for people who have done the job before, there are certainly other criteria to consider. For example, have they seen it done, can they describe how it is done, and are they agile learners? Some who have done the job before are bored with it and may not be as interested as someone newer to the task. Also, if everything else lines up, you might want to choose the candidate for whom this is new or a stretch, especially if the missing skills are readily trainable.

Assumption: He is too old or too young for this job.

Fact: What's age got to do with it? Architect Frank Lloyd Wright and heart surgeon Michael DeBakey are examples of people who excelled in their crafts after the age of 90.

Assumption: We need a man in this job because it is too emotionally challenging for a woman.

Fact: The ability to function well is made up of a combination of traits, skills, behaviors, and experience that is *gender-neutral* (meaning gender does not predict ability).

When you find yourself forming assumptions about candidates based on their gender or size or color (and, by the way, we all do that sometimes), then gently move yourself back to the key criteria you have identified and your methodology for assessing all of your candidates fairly.

Orient and Support

Too often we choose the right people but fail to support them as they assume their new roles. Maybe that's why so many people leave within the first year on the job. Orientation and support are key pieces of the selection process and will ensure that you increase the odds of their success and contribution to the team.

Recruiting top talent is tough, but keeping top talent can be an even bigger challenge. Studies show that most new employees who quit do so within the first three months of employment. Common reasons cited are frustration with procedures or unmet expectations.

Usually, it is not an unwillingness of management or staff to smooth the way for new workers, but more of a time crunch quandary. Most companies are streamlined to the max, and taking time to properly indoctrinate new workers on procedures can rob existing staff of valuable production time. This leaves newcomers in an unfortunate sink or swim position.[19]

Several organizations we know are requiring their managers to have a series of conversations with their new hires over at least the first year. The purpose of these conversations is to continually address the employees' needs as well as those of the organization. In addition, the conversations are designed to build the relationship between the manager and the new hire.

Alas

I've left a few companies after being there only three months. In a couple of cases, the projects turned out much less interesting or challenging than management had described. In one particularly bad case, I was told about a system that would have been really interesting, but once I got there and actually started talking with them about the details, I found out that the things they described to me weren't even possible for nontechnical reasons. The system actually was just a data entry Web site.

Another time, as a contractor, I was brought in to do software development. Instead, they put me on production support. When my contract was up three months later I chose, to their dismay, not to continue the contract.

Now I don't trust what they tell me about the position, but other than ask a lot of questions, I can't really do much.

—Software engineer

Here are some questions that you may want to use with your own new recruits:

1. Are we delivering what we promised? What are we delivering on? What are we not delivering on?
2. What kind of support or direction do you need from me that you aren't getting? What are you getting that you don't want?
3. How are you developing relationships with colleagues? Are you finding people to go to lunch with? Are you finding people to go to when you need help?[20]

Isn't orientation something the human resources department handles? Maybe so—when teaching the overall company policies and procedures. But you, the manager, get to do the rest. Better yet, involve your team in the process.

TO DO . . .

✓ Have an "expectations exchange" with your new employees. Clearly define what you expect from them and ask what they are expecting from you and the team.

✓ Spend time teaching them about the organization they have just joined. Tell stories, sharing your experiences and knowledge about the culture and history.

✓ Involve your key people in the new hires' orientation. Expose new employees to others' views and stories as well as your own.

✓ Mentor and find mentors for them as they work to close the inevitable skill gaps (those you no doubt identified in the interview process).

✓ Treat them well and introduce them to others on your team even before their first day. People with several options could be tempted by another offer before they show up for the first day of work!

✓ Be available to support them in this uncertain early stage of their employment. That may mean seeking them out to see how they are doing and conveying that you are behind them all the way.

Re-Recruit as Well

A successful accountant, tragically killed by a speeding bus, arrives at the Pearly Gates and is welcomed by St. Peter. St. Peter explains that she will need to spend one day in Heaven and one day in Hell before she decides where she would like to spend eternity.

With great trepidation she enters Hell and is amazed to find a beautiful golf course, friends and colleagues who welcome her, terrific food, a great party, and even a nice-guy devil. At the end of her day, she regretfully leaves Hell in order to experience her day in Heaven. That experience is quite good also, with the clouds, angels, harps, and singing that she expected.

St. Peter pushes her to make the decision of a lifetime (and beyond). In which place would she spend eternity—Heaven or Hell? You guessed it—she chooses Hell. When she returns to Hell, she finds a desolate wasteland and her friends dressed in rags, picking up garbage. There are no parties—only misery and despair. She says to the Devil, "I don't understand. Yesterday I was here and there was a golf course and a country club, we ate lobster, and we danced and had a great time. Now I see a wasteland and all my friends look miserable." The Devil looks at her and smiles. "Yesterday we were recruiting you; today you're an employee."

If you chuckled knowingly at this story, it may be because there is a shred (or more) of truth to it. You may have experienced it yourself— the wining and dining during the recruitment phase (it's almost like courting), and then a cold, cruel reality once you signed on. If your new hire faces cold reality too soon, you will surely lose that new gem. Research shows that you actually re-recruit your new hires for the first year of their employment and that they are easily enticed away during that time.

But what about the rest of your talent? While you are busy hiring the best-fit candidates for key roles on your team, do a little re-recruiting along the way. Often candidates and new employees are viewed as close to perfect (their warts haven't surfaced yet), and they get all the attention.

If you have done a great job of selecting, you will have a whole new stable of stars. Your long-term employees can feel less noticed, less appreciated, and perhaps even taken for granted as you carefully select, orient, and train these new folks. Avoid that dangerous phenomenon by re-recruiting your talent. Show your current employees that they are important and critical to you and to the success of your team, especially as you recruit new team members.

If you're not recruiting your best people, you're the only one who isn't.

BOTTOM LINE

Great managers are great recruiters. The best never take down their "Help Wanted" sign. Remember that *fit is it* when it comes to hiring. If you get the right people in the right roles in your organization and on your team, you absolutely will increase the odds of retaining them.

Chapter 9

INFORMATION

Share It

*I never felt like I was really a part of the organization . . . I mean,
I often read about what we were doing in the news!*

—A.J.

We live in an information age. Powerful new businesses exist solely for
the purpose of leading you to the information you want. That reality has
changed people's attitudes towards sharing or hoarding information.

*The Web will change relationships with employees. We will never again
have discussions where knowledge is hidden in somebody's pocket.
You will have to lead with ideas, not by controlling information.*
    —Jack Welch, former CEO, General Electric

So what's the big deal about information? In this busy, time-crunched
environment, you simply may not have time to share information with
your employees. What if you don't?

First: It's hard for you to do your best without good information.
The same is true for your employees.

Second: You will lose your talent—maybe not today, but eventually those with choices will leave you.

Having the Scoop or Out of the Loop

Information is power. But you've known that for a long time. As kids we knew that having the inside scoop is cool, and we felt important if we were given information that others did not have. If information is power, then being out of the loop—lacking information—might leave one powerless. Research shows that people want a boss with influence and power in the organization.[21] Think about your own work experience, and you will probably agree that you would much rather work for someone who is in the loop than for a boss who is clueless. Your employees are no different. They want you to be in the loop, and they want and need you to bring them in too.

In the Absence of Information, They Will Make It Up

Information sharing during dramatic change is even more critical than during stable times. We have seen dozens of examples of high-level managers deciding to withhold information in organizations going through major change (downsizing, mergers, acquisitions). We've seen middle managers hoarding information out of fear of losing their power or importance. We acknowledge that at times you simply cannot share, but check out what might happen when you withhold information about change:

Senior Manager Thinks	Employees Think
It's too early to tell them.	Silence must mean it's pretty bad.
This news is too frightening—we'd better wait.	They're moving the company to Panama.
I'm afraid if we tell them, productivity will drop.	The company's going belly-up. Where else can I get a job?

Notice that the manager is trying to protect the employees and prevent all the water cooler talk that can put a huge dent in productivity. Ironically, the silence and protection backfire. Productivity plummets as these employees worry about their jobs and update their resumés.

In contrast, where top leaders give information as early and honestly as possible and hold managers accountable for passing the news down, employees actually feel important and valued, and the productivity dip is minimized.

Another good reason to share information is that your employees might be able to help. A major hospital offers a good example:

The hospital had a policy of never eliminating positions through layoffs—a commitment it had kept throughout its history, including its merger with another hospital. Several years ago, the policy was tested when the hospital faced a potential $20 million deficit. Management shared the news with the staff and asked for their help. Within 10 days, they received 4,000 cost-saving ideas from employees. Sixteen task forces formed to deal with the ideas. While most of the strategies involved tighter controls on purchasing, employees also suggested forgoing raises and holding off on accrued paid time off. By the end of the year, the task forces had realized enough savings to eliminate the need for layoffs.

Getting Your Fair Share

So how do you know what and how much to share? The answer is, it depends. It depends primarily on your organization's culture and management philosophy. At one end of the openness continuum lies the philosophy of Jack Stack, founder of Springfield Remanufacturing Company (SRC) in Springfield, Missouri. He wrote *The Great Game of Business* and *A Stake in the Outcome,* and espouses "open book management," a set of beliefs and business practices that dozens of highly successful organizations have adopted. He says, "We are building a company in which everyone tells the truth every day—not because everyone is honest, but because everyone has access to the same information: operating metrics, financial data, valuation estimates. The more people understand what's really going on in their company, the more eager they are to help solve its problems."[22] It's clear that when Jack Stack says "open book," he means tell it all!

You may not work in such an information-open environment, but consider the consequences of your communication style and the culture in which you manage. Do what you can to share information with your employees. You'll increase commitment and enhance the odds of keeping your best people.

No, You Don't Need a Crystal Ball

see CAREER

You are expected to help your team look to the future. That includes providing information that supports your employees' development and career advancement. You need to share what you know about

- ✓ Your organization's strategic direction and goals,
- ✓ Your profession, industry, and organization's future,
- ✓ The emerging trends and new developments that may affect career possibilities, and
- ✓ The cultural and political realities of your organization.

As you forecast, your team members will learn to look broadly at their profession, industry, and organization and see the trends and implications. They will also feel more competent and confident in their future marketability.

TO DO . . .

- ✓ Forward articles that relate to your industry for your employees to read. You probably have access to industry-based newsletters, reports, and magazines that they may never see. You'll share critical information that can help them make decisions about their career development.

Have you ever had a boss tell you, "I knew that weeks ago, but couldn't (or decided not to) share it with you"? Isn't that infuriating? You may have thought: "Thanks a lot. A lot of good this does me now!" or "See if I trust you in the future," or "Why even tell me you knew? Is this a power trip?"

A CEO accepted the resignation of a member of his senior team and knew there would be an impact on the organization. When we asked him when he planned to share that information with his key players, he responded, "I don't want to upset them during a tense time, so I think I'll wait until our staff meeting in two days."

What do you think? Good idea? No, bad idea. What are the odds that people wouldn't find out about the resignation the same day? People knew within the hour and were frustrated, disappointed, and even angry that the CEO had not informed them immediately. Many felt distrusted, even undervalued by their boss as a result of his nondisclosure.

Alas

We were working on a large Department of Defense program and spent hours preparing for a major "proof of concept" demonstration. In the meantime, our boss was in higher-level discussions with the client, in which the client shared the fact that the entire program was going through a big funding review and that the plug might be pulled before the demonstration took place. We didn't hear about it until the day of the demonstration. Then we learned how close we had come to the demonstration never taking place. We felt disenfranchised and undervalued. Had he shared the seriousness of the situation with us, we could have produced other supporting arguments and generated other scenarios that would have helped our client to support the program with his superiors.

(continued)

> *Our boss probably thought he was shielding us from things we didn't need to worry about, or he thought we wouldn't give 100 percent if we knew about this conversation. He didn't place much value on our ability to contribute; it felt paternalistic and elitist. After that, my trust level with my manager was never the same. I think the whole team felt the same way.*
>
> —Senior engineer, civil engineering firm

An absence of communication can breed anxiety and paranoia, which leads to high turnover rates, gossip, and in some cases angst among once-harmonious colleagues.[23]

So, as a manager, when should you share information? *The sooner the better!* When you are clear about what you want or need to share, find a way to do it soon, especially if the information is about a major change. Here are some *trigger events* that might alert you to the need for information-giving:

✓ Merger or acquisition

✓ On-line or print article about the company

✓ A requisition for a key position

✓ New hires

✓ An overactive rumor mill

How to Share

Remember that the primary focus of this book is how to keep your talented employees. Volumes have been written about communication strategies, both in normal times and during times of dramatic change. Face-to-face communication, video, newsletter, e-mail, voice mail, open forums, and bulletin boards all have their place in communicating effectively. Our question is, Which approach works best, given your organization's culture and the message you are trying to send?

Here are a few guidelines:

TO DO...

✓ Share information face-to-face, especially if it is difficult to deliver or will affect your employees significantly. Tell your direct reports the news yourself, rather than having them learn it via memo or from some other source. Let your supervisors give the news to their direct reports also. Research shows that people believe it and react more favorably when the news is delivered in this manner. If it has to travel through several layers, double-check to be sure the message is getting through.

✓ Get creative. The more creatively you send a message, the greater the chance your employees will notice it. Consider doing the unexpected. If people are used to hearing news via e-mail, try face-to-face or video next time.

Close to the Vest?

Building an information-rich culture can be challenging. After all, there will be times when you are privy to information that you simply cannot share with your employees. A few simple guidelines can help you handle the situation appropriately without alienating your employees. When the information must be held in confidence, keep these tips in mind:

✓ Don't share, no matter how tempting the information might be.
✓ Never use information withholding as a power tool. If you are given proprietary or "secret" information, do not tell people you have it unless they ask you.
✓ If people ask you if you have information, be honest. Don't tell them you don't have information when you do.
✓ Tell them that you are not at liberty to share, and tell them why; for example, "The information is sensitive or proprietary," or "I have

been asked to keep it confidential, and I need to honor that request."

✓ Be prepared for the possibility that your responses may not please people, and some may feel that you really should or could tell them if you wanted to. If you establish a track record of early, honest information-sharing, you will have more room to withhold information when the situation dictates.

It's a Two-Way Street

Getting information is also a way of keeping your employees. People want to be heard regarding their jobs, the work at hand, and the organization's goals and strategies. As a manager, you need to ask for that input.

> *When I started visiting the plants and meeting with employees, what was reassuring was the tremendous, positive energy in our conversations. One man said he had been with the company for 25 years and hated every minute of it—until he was asked for his opinion. He said that question transformed his job.*
>
> —CEO, Big-3 auto manufacturer

While most managers expect employees to come to them if there is a problem, often employees don't feel comfortable or managers don't offer the opportunity. Help your employees feel comfortable talking to you by scheduling regular opportunities for those talks.

BOTTOM LINE

Stay in the loop. Keep your employees in the loop. It will help you keep your talent.

Chapter 10

ERK

Don't Be One

I know one department that kept losing talented people, one after the other. It was no mystery really. The manager was a complete jerk.

—A.J.

—WARNING—
If this book landed on your desk with a bookmark here, pay attention!

People cautioned us not to write this chapter, or at least not to use this title. But to avoid this topic is to avoid discussing a primary reason why people leave their jobs. If employees don't like their bosses, they will leave even when they are well paid, receive recognition, and have a chance to learn and grow. In fact, disliking the boss is one of the top causes of talent loss. Take a look at this exit interview:

Interviewer: Mathew, why have you decided to leave the organization? I know that we pay competitively and you just received a bonus.

Mathew: Is this confidential?

Interviewer: Definitely, yes.

Mathew: The pay is fine. The work is fine. But my boss is impossible. He is so difficult to work with, and I've decided life is too short to spend it working for a jerk.

Have you ever worked for a jerk? Are there any jerks in your organization? In a poll of 50,000 visitors to www.careerbuilder.com and www.msn.com, one in three polled described their boss as "a nightmare," and an additional 11 percent said more gently that their boss was "difficult to work with." Another study reported that after 20 years of research and 60,000 exit interviews, 80 percent of turnover can be related to unsatisfactory relationships with the boss.[24]

We've received dozens of "jerk" stories from our readers. Here are some of the toppers.

Alas after Alas

✓ *"My boss told me I was passed over for promotion because I hadn't gotten over my grief soon enough following my father's death."*

✓ *"My boss told me to come talk to him anytime. I went in for a topic important to me: my career. He kept reading (even answering) his e-mail while I talked. Guess how important I felt."*

✓ *"My first job out of college, my boss wanted me to cancel my vacation when the client requested deadline changes. However, he wouldn't cancel his trip to Greece!"*

✓ *"The boss I refer to as 'Mr. Toxic' told me in a memo that I was getting too fat to represent the company professionally."*

✓ *"I had a boss who would drop his pencil on my side of the desk when I was pregnant. He thought it was funny to watch me struggle to pick it up."*

✓ *"Prior to a meeting my boss said, 'You take charge, run the meeting, assert your authority.' During the meeting, the boss continually interrupted, contradicted, and undermined my authority, even though I followed our pre-set agenda."*

(continued)

> ✓ *"The dentist I worked for actually threw instruments at me when I wasn't fast enough in assisting him. Our patients were horrified, and many left our practice because of it."*
>
> ✓ *"My boss put two talented employees on a 30-day suspension because they left work to go home and check on their kids immediately following a 7.0 earthquake in Seattle. He, by the way, had already checked in with his wife and knew his kids were fine."*

Hard to believe, huh? Or maybe not. Unfortunately, most of us have worked for a jerk at some point in our lives. Most of us escaped!

This chapter is not about labeling people as jerks and letting the rest of us off the hook. It is about defining jerk-like behaviors and the "jerk mode" that people occasionally assume. It is about learning to assess whether or not you exhibit those behaviors and how often. And it's about trying to change for the better. Why? To engage, motivate, and keep your talented people.

To learn more about jerk-like behavior, go to our website, www.keepem. com and take the Jerk Survey.

What Is a Jerk?

We asked dozens of people, "What do jerks act like or look like?" This checklist reflects what we heard.[25] We dare you to score yourself.

Behavior Checklist

Instructions: Score yourself on the following behaviors, using a 0–5 scale: 0 means you never act this way, and 5 means you often act this way.

	0–5
Intimidate	_____
Condescend or demean	_____
Act arrogant	_____
Withhold praise	_____

Slam doors, pound tables	_____
Swear	_____
Behave rudely	_____
Belittle people in front of others	_____
Micromanage	_____
Manage up, not down	_____
Always look out for number one	_____
Give mostly negative feedback	_____
Yell at people	_____
Tell lies or "half-truths"	_____
Act above the rules	_____
Enjoy making people sweat	_____
Act superior to or smarter than everyone else	_____
Show disrespect	_____
Act sexist	_____
Act bigoted	_____
Withhold critical information	_____
Use inappropriate humor	_____
Blow up in meetings	_____
Start every sentence with "I"	_____
Steal credit or the spotlight from others	_____
Block career moves (prevent promotion or hold onto "stars")	_____
Distrust most people	_____
Show favoritism	_____
Humiliate and embarrass others	_____
Criticize often (at a personal level)	_____
Overuse sarcasm	_____
Deliberately ignore or isolate some people	_____
Set impossible goals or deadlines	_____
Never accept blame, let others take the hit	_____
Undermine authority	_____
Show lack of caring for people	_____
Betray trust or confidences	_____

Gossip/spread rumors	_____
Act as if others are stupid	_____
Have "sloppy moods" (when feeling down, take it out on others)	_____
Use fear as a motivator	_____
Show revenge	_____
Interrupt constantly	_____
Make "bad-taste" remarks	_____
Fail to listen	_____
Lack patience	_____
Demand perfection	_____
Break promises	_____
Second-guess constantly	_____
Have to always be in control	_____
Total score:	_____

Note: This assessment is a tool to help give you some insight, not a validated instrument. The following interpretation guidelines are just that—guidelines.

Interpretation Guidelines

0–20   Although you have a bad day now and then, you are probably not viewed as a jerk. Watch those behaviors for which you scored above a 3, and get more feedback from your employees.

21–60   Look out! You could be viewed as a jerk by some, at least in some situations. Commit to reading and implementing two or more chapters in this book.

61 or more   You are at high risk for losing talent. Get more feedback and consider getting a coach.

If you checked none of the behaviors on this assessment, either you're a saint, or you have a few blind spots. In other words, most of us do exhibit some of these behaviors some of the time. The question is, how many and how often? And what effect does your behavior have on the people who report to you?

Warren Bennis gave his view of the Jayson Blair firing from the New York Times *for dishonesty. "It doesn't matter how many prizes you win if you damage your real prize—your talent—in the process. Uncaring, arrogant leadership that values accolades at any cost is always inappropriate, but especially ill-suited to idea-driven organizations such as the* Times. *Whatever their titles or official positions, talented people have their own power. They have the power to walk. They will not stay in an organization that treats them like cattle, even if the name on the building is as august as the* New York Times. *Raines and his more imperious predecessors polarized their staffs and made them compete with each other for newsroom resources, including the favor of the executive editor. Such intramural competition ends up making people less creative, not more creative."*

Bennis pointed out that part of the problem was the leadership of the executive editor, Howell Raines. "Raines was an ego-driven autocrat who ruled by fear, played favorites, had an idiosyncratic news judgment, and loathed hearing unwanted truths."[26]

Who, Me?

Give your results from the jerk checklist some serious thought. Ask your friends at work to look at the list with you and give you honest feedback. (If you don't have any friends, that may be a clue.) Ask family members to give you insight as well. If others agree that you *often* exhibit more than one or two of those behaviors, you are at high risk for losing talent. Jerk-like behaviors are so damaging that even one or two can negate all of your other strengths as a boss.

I had no idea that my employees viewed me as such a jerk. We had 360-degree feedback (input from boss, peers, subordinates, even cus-

tomers) as a part of a leadership development program. Employees had a chance to type in comments at the end of a lengthy computerized survey. My employees basically told me that I came across as insensitive and uncaring. They said that my drive to get results seemed to be at any cost, including employee health and morale. I was so shocked at this feedback. I felt terrible. Now I'm working with a coach to help me figure out how to change my behaviors. The first step was finding out how my employees viewed me.

—Senior manager, engineering firm

If you have never had an in-depth *360-degree feedback* assessment, consider it. The feedback should come to you anonymously, and it should be used for your own awareness and development. Recognizing your ineffective and potentially damaging behaviors is the first step to doing something about them.

see TRUTH

Once a Jerk, Always a Jerk?

Just as you can learn new leadership skills at any age, you can stop ineffective behaviors or replace them with more effective ones.

I used to blow up at people. When I was under stress, and someone said the wrong thing, I just lost control. I yelled, turned red in the face, and pounded the table. The result was that people used to tiptoe around me. They hid bad news and took few risks, fearing my temper if they failed. People were intimidated. We lost creativity, productivity, and some talent along the way—all because of my uncontrolled temper.

Now I'm better, at least 90 percent of the time. It took some time and a lot of effort, but I now have a handle on my emotions. When I feel the blood pressure rise and my anger coming on, I picture a stop sign. I stop, take three slow, deep breaths, and then we talk about the problem. What a difference—both in how I feel about myself and how my employees react.

—Manager, marketing and sales department

Because behaviors are learned, we know that it is possible to change. It may not be easy, but it is possible. The difficulty of changing ineffective behaviors depends on the answers to several questions:

✓ How ingrained is the behavior? Have you been acting this way for 50 years or for three? Some of those long-term habits are certainly more difficult to break than those more recently learned.

✓ Are you crystal-clear about what the desired behavior will look like? A clear picture of the goal will certainly make it easier to get there.

✓ Do you have resources available to help you? It's easier to change if you have people supporting you.

✓ How complex is the behavior? You may be able to decide simply to stop telling off-color jokes and never do it again. Negative reactions under stress are more complicated and interwoven, so they will probably require more focus, more resources, and a longer time to change. You may need to develop a new repertoire of behaviors from which to choose.

✓ Do you really want to change? Why? If you can't answer this question, you will not change. You've got to want to.

Once you decide to change, you can create your action plan.

When he was CEO of PepsiCo, Andy Pearson was named one of the toughest bosses in America, based on his ability to inflict pain and humiliation. He brought talented people to tears with his words and proved he was smart by finding fault with other people's ideas. He was heard saying to key employees, "A room full of monkeys could do better than this!" Pearson realized late in life that he could be more effective if he led differently. He now seeks answers and ideas from employees at all levels, rather than issuing orders. He believes his job is to listen to the people who work for him and to serve them. Today he says, "It's all about having more genuine concern for the other person. There's a big difference between being tough and being tough-minded. There's an important aspect of leading that has to do with humility." Pearson made these changes in his 70s. Even "old dogs" can learn new tricks—if they really want to! [27]

TO DO . . .

✓ Get honest feedback somehow. You need a clear picture of how you look to others.

✓ Ask, "So what?" Think about the implications of your behaviors. Are they getting in the way of your effectiveness? Are they causing good people to leave?

✓ Take a stress management course.

✓ Exercise. Eat well. Sleep more. You choose.

✓ Try tai chi, yoga, meditation, or prayer.

✓ If you decide to change, seek help from others:

- Get a coach.
- Seek counseling.
- Attend a personal growth seminar.
- Read self-improvement books.
- Ask people to monitor and give you feedback as you attempt to change.

BOTTOM LINE

If you believe (or find out) that you often exhibit jerk-like behaviors, decide to change. This book exists to help you do it. Changing jerk-like behaviors may be the most important action you can take to keep your talent on your team.

Chapter 11

KICKS

Get Some

My boss held the "all work, no play" philosophy. Work was simply not the place for fun.

—A.J.

How do you feel about fun at work? Do you believe in it? Have it? Support it? Make it happen? Discourage it? Evaluate your own assumptions about fun at work. Then consider creating and supporting kicks in the workplace as one way to keep your best people.

Research shows that a fun-filled workplace generates enthusiasm—and that enthusiasm leads to increased productivity, better customer service, a positive attitude about the company, and higher odds that your talent will stay.

In today's uncertain work environment, humor isn't an option, it's a necessary way to boost morale. When employees clown around, they're not wasting valuable time, they're making use of one of the few tools available to increase and maintain their esprit de corps. Laughter may not change the external reality, but it can certainly help people survive it.[28]

Fun for One—Fun for All?

When was the last time you had a good laugh at work?

✓ Last year?
✓ Last month?
✓ Last week?
✓ Yesterday?

If your answer was yesterday, you're probably smiling as you read this.

Of course, one person's fun can be another person's turnoff. Telling jokes may be fun for you and ridiculous (or even insulting) to someone else. Some people get kicks out of decorating your office as a birthday surprise, while others love to take a break to debate some current hot topic or to surf the Web. So remember to ask people, "What makes work more fun?"

see ASK

> *Humorize, and you humanize the workplace.*
> —Fran Solomon, senior vice empress, Playfair, Inc.

Fun-Free Zone

Unfortunately, many workplaces are fun-free zones. In one study, workers graded their bosses on the degree to which they supported or allowed fun at work. The average grade was a measly C+.[29] If you're one of those C+ bosses and you are not having or allowing fun at work, why is that? Maybe you just were not raised that way. The bosses you learned from may have been fun-averse, serious taskmasters. Perhaps you believe that allowing fun at work will cause you to lose control or fail to achieve results. You might think that moments of levity will set bad precedents, and the group will never get back to business. Some of your concerns may be based on *fun myths* about having kicks in the workplace.

TO DO . . .

Check which of these myths you tend to believe in:

✓ Myth #1: Professionalism and fun are incompatible.
✓ Myth #2: It takes toys and money to have fun.
✓ Myth #3: Fun means laughter.
✓ Myth #4: You have to plan for fun.
✓ Myth #5: Fun time at work will compromise our results.
✓ Myth #6: You have to have a good sense of humor (or be funny) to create a fun work environment.

Myth Debunking

These myths are just that—myths. Let's debunk them.

Myth #1: Professionalism and Fun Are Incompatible.

Can you have fun and still maintain a professional work environment? It depends on the kind of fun you are talking about. Slapstick silliness (pie-in-the-face humor) will not fit well in a business-suit environment. But there are many appropriate ways to get some kicks in even the most buttoned-up workplace.

> *Every month we had client reports due and most of us dreaded the solitary extra-hours work that the task required. So we started planning to stay late one night each month. We went to a deli for snacks and good wine and then held a work party. We were all on our own computers in our own offices, but we took regular breaks, helped each other, enjoyed our food and wine together, and had some laughs in the after-work casual environment. It not only made the monthly task much more enjoyable, but it provided a type of team building.*
> —Consultant, management consulting firm

In another highly professional work environment, when someone is late to a meeting, they either have to sing a song or tell a new joke (in good taste!). People are on time more often since the new rule, but there is also a guaranteed chuckle as people slide in the door a minute or two late.

Most concern about having fun in a serious workplace is actually concern about inappropriate humor, loud behavior, or poor timing. If employees' timing is off or their behavior is embarrassing or disruptive, give them that feedback, just as you would about any work behaviors.

Myth #2: It Takes Toys and Money to Have Fun at Work.

This is the sister myth to "It takes toys and money to have fun in life." When we asked dozens of people to reflect on fun times they remembered having at work, here is what we heard. (Notice how many of these examples cost money or involve toys.)

✓ "No specific time. It was just the day-to-day laughter my colleagues and I shared—mostly about small things."

✓ "We decorated my boss's office for his birthday. We used five bags of confetti from the shredding machine."

✓ "Spontaneous after-work trips to the local pizza parlor."

✓ "Verbal sparring with my brainy, funny colleagues."

✓ "When we had a huge project, a tight deadline, and we had to work all night. I wouldn't want to do that often, but we had a good time, laughs in the middle of the night, and a thrill when we finished the project."

✓ "Receiving this poem from my dedicated, funny employees whom I sent to Detroit on business: 'Roses are red, violets are blue, it's 30 below, and we hate you.'"

✓ "In the midst of a big stressful project, our boss took us to a local park for a volleyball game during lunch. We still talk about it."

Toys and money certainly can help you have fun too. Microsoft and Amgen are two large companies with "fun" budgets. In both companies, people are expected to work hard and play hard. Their play includes the occasional extravagant party or boat trip. Although employees greatly appreciate elaborate outings, most report that it is the day-to-day work environment that matters most. It has to be enjoyable.

Myth #3: Fun Means Laughter.

Fun often does involve laughter or smiles. Sometimes people just need to take themselves less seriously.

> *We have to be so intellectual most of the time. We like to occasionally go off into silliness.*
>
> —Math professor and her tutors

Laughter has been called *internal jogging,* as it has the same positive health benefit as an aerobic run. Supposedly this works through the release of endorphins, the healing elements of the body.

But people can have fun at work without laughing or getting silly. An intriguing project and collaboration with wonderful teammates can truly be fun. Work that is meaningful and makes a difference can be fun. Building something new can be fun.

> *Some of the most fun I ever had was in the early days of creating a completely new form of airplane. We were building something new that would make a difference. It was difficult and challenging but so much fun.*
>
> —Retired aeronautical engineer

Myth #4: You Have to Plan for Fun.

Planned fun makes sense sometimes. The employee softball team provides fun and requires planning, as does an occasional employee picnic or the annual holiday party. But a lot of fun in the workplace is spontaneous.

> *We had been working so hard and had nailed all of our goals for the quarter. My boss called us into his office and presented the team with movie tickets—for the two o'clock show, that day! It was great. We*

took off as a group and felt like kids, playing hooky from school. It was so spontaneous and so appreciated.

—City government employee

Unplanned fun can be as simple as showing up at the staff meeting with muffins for everyone, asking a group of employees to join you for lunch at a new restaurant, or taking an unplanned coffee break to just sit and talk about families or hobbies.

If you do want to surprise your team and plan some fun, keep these two lists in mind.[34]

Top Ten Most Popular Foods
10. *Beer (champagne, wine)*
 9. *Candy bars*
 8. *Pretzels (to go with the beer)*
 7. *M&Ms*
 6. *Cake*
 5. *Popcorn*
 4. *Ice Cream*
 3. *Doughnuts*
 2. *Pizza*
 1. *Cookies (the overwhelming choice)*

Top Ten Most Popular Office Toys
10. *Pogo sticks or hula hoops*
 9. *Yo-yos*
 8. *Tinkertoys*
 7. *Slinky*
 6. *Pez dispensers*
 5. *Frisbees*
 4. *Silly Putty*
 3. *Nerf balls*
 2. *Nerf guns*
 1. *Koosh balls*

Myth #5: Fun Time at Work Will Compromise Results.

This is one of managers' largest concerns. Somehow many of them feel that every minute spent chuckling is a minute lost toward bottom-line results.

Alas

Somehow three of us stepped out of our offices at the same time, met in the hallway, and began chatting. I don't even remember what we began laughing about, but all three of us were really laughing (not very quietly). Our boss stepped out of his office with a furious, red-faced look and said, "Is this what I'm paying you for?" We were embarrassed, humiliated, and angry. I left the company shortly after that, as did the other two people. It was a stifling environment where fun was not allowed. Ten years later, I still remember that incident.

—Retail sales manager

Research verifies that fun-loving environments are actually more productive than their humorless counterparts. A fun break can reenergize your employees and ready them for the next concentrated effort. In one Microsoft group, employees take breaks whenever they want by surfing the Web or playing games on their computers. They say that these playful activities clear their minds so that when they return to the project at hand, they are fresher and sharper.

If you aren't having fun in your work, fix the problem before it becomes serious: ask for help if you need it. If you can't fix it and won't ask for help, please go away before you spoil the fun for the rest of us.

—Russ Walden

You might be thinking, "If I allow my employees to surf the Web during work, they will never get their work done." Maybe you believe that only exceptional employees can be trusted to that degree. The secret to allowing fun at work is to be *crystal-clear* with your employees about their performance goals. Co-create measurable and specific goals with them, then evaluate their performance using those goals.

Some of the most productive, successful organizations in the world are renowned for fun. Southwest Airlines Chairman of the Board Herb Kelleher set the famous Southwest tone. He has loaded baggage on Thanksgiving Day, ridden his Harley Davidson motorcycle into company headquarters, and golfed at the Southwest golf tournament with just one club. He even arm-wrestled another CEO for the rights to an advertising slogan. Southwest flight attendants get their kicks by singing the departure instructions to their passengers. All this fun and they still please shareholders and win major airline awards.[31]

Myth #6: You Have to Have a Good Sense of Humor (or Be Funny) to Create a Fun Work Environment.

You may not be like Herb Kelleher. Many terrific bosses are not necessarily funny (or even very fun-loving). In many cases, they simply allow others' humor and playfulness to come out. They *support* rather than create fun at work. Let others initiate the kicks if fun is not your strength.

> My favorite boss was not necessarily a fun-loving person. She was pretty task-oriented and serious most of the time. One time she did dress up for Halloween, and we were all completely shocked. That was a real stretch for her. Most of the time she just let us have our fun, without judging or squelching it.
>
> —Supervisor, hospital

You might bring fun into your workplace by having brown bag lunches with interesting speakers and topics. During a hobby-sharing lunch, one employee took everyone to a local park to demonstrate his remote-controlled airplanes. Another brought a local merchant to give a session on wine tasting. Another invited the local golf pro to give everyone a lesson.

Funny Makes Money

Fun breeds creativity. Add a little fun to the work environment, and energy goes up. With that, productivity goes up. With that, innovation goes up. With that, new ideas are developed and money comes in. (Well, it's not *quite* that simple. But it happens.)

> *Managers at Irvine-based Fluor Corp. invited a group of gifted children from a local school to a management training meeting. The children sat with one group of executives, while a second group of Fluor managers worked independently. At day's end, the mixed group of executives and children had generated far more innovative ideas than the executives-only group.*[32]

BOTTOM LINE

Experience in companies of all sizes proves it: fun enhances creativity, and it does not diminish productivity when work goals are clear. Let fun happen. That fun will energize, motivate, and keep talented people on your team.

Chapter 12

LINK

Create Connections

I just didn't feel very connected. In the time I was there, I never had much opportunity to meet anyone outside of my immediate work unit. And my work unit seemed to be made up of a lot of lone rangers.

—A.J.

Is your organization easy to leave? It's easy to leave a workplace

✓ Where you feel no connection;
✓ Where you have no group of colleagues who can offer support, information, or plain old gripe sessions;
✓ If it is difficult to move your ideas through the pipeline;
✓ If you do not have relationships that help you get your work done;
✓ If you don't look forward to seeing the people with whom you interact;
✓ If you don't feel proud of or don't understand the organization's mission and purpose.

Are You a Linker or NonLinker?

A *nonlinker* thinks, "If I link my employees to other functions or departments, someone there will steal them."

A *linker* thinks, "If I don't link my employees to other functions or departments, their knowledge and skills are less likely to grow. My employees' productivity will be limited to the resources of their own department. Their work may become too function focused for overall success, and I won't be as connected as I need to be, either."

> *Networking: An arrangement of people crossed at regular intervals by other people, all of whom are cultivating mutually beneficial, give-and-take, win-win relationships with each other.*
>
> *Just as we are all at the center of our own particular universe, we are also at the center of our network. We realize, of course, that all the other people are at the center of their network, and that is how it should be.*
>
> *Each of the people in this network serve as a source of support (referrals, help, information, etc.) for everyone else in that network. Those who know how to use the tremendous strength of a network realize this very important fact: We are not dependent on each other; nor are we independent of each other; we are all interdependent with each other.*
>
> —Bob Burg, author of *Endless Referrals*

A *linker* knows that in our high-speed culture, no employee can do the job well without connections. Speed, quality, and quantity of output depend on strong networks. The more individuals feel they can draw on resourceful colleagues, the more likely they are to stay.

Where can you start building links between your employees and various communities? Link 'em to

- ✓ The organization as a whole.
- ✓ The team or department.
- ✓ The professional community.
- ✓ The local community.

Linking to the Organization

> *No matter what business you're in, everyone in the organization needs to know why.*
>
> —Frances Hesselbein, president, The Drucker Foundation

You don't need to work for the American Red Cross or Greenpeace to build a meaningful connection between an employee and the organization. An article in the *World at Work Journal* states that a critical retention success driver is "how well employees understand the company's mission, strategies and goals and how they can contribute to company results. Companies that fail to educate employees on business and organizational objectives, and customer needs often have higher turnover rates."[33]

As a manager there is much you can do to create the link. Sometimes all it takes is a discussion about the history of the company, its founders, its reason for being, the important needs it meets, or what customers say the company has done for them through its product line or service.

One medical device manufacturer brought in patients from a local hospital whose lives were saved or enhanced thanks to the company's product. All employees at all levels attended these meetings and were able to ask questions of these users. Employees swelled with pride and deepened their link to the organization.

Meetings with the president, CEO, or other senior leaders are critical to linking employees with an organization's purpose. While mission statements capture the underlying principles of the organization and seldom change, the goals of the organization are dynamic. Keep employees abreast of these organization-wide changes to help them feel connected. If employees hear about changes (good or bad) in passing, they may feel out of the loop and start the dreaded rumor mill.

The Federal Reserve Bank of New York helps people connect within the organization with a social group called the Federal Reserve Club. It sponsors trips in which employees of all functions, titles, and levels may participate. This gives employees who wouldn't normally interact daily the opportunity to talk with each other informally. When an employee needs some information from another department, it's likely that he or she will have a contact and won't be afraid to pick up the phone.

see OPPORTUNITIES

One way to find organizational links is to list all the interdepartmental meetings you attend in a week. (Does the list give you a headache?)

Which ones could you delegate to a member of your team? You will even free up some time on your own schedule.

How do you create a bond among the employees in the department and increase the chances of deepening their loyalty? There are many ways.

TO DO . . .

✓ Have open forum meetings on a regular basis. If employees feel they are being heard, they will feel a stronger connection to you and the group. Don't be afraid of grievances, either. Even if you can't do anything to fix a problem, people feel better just having the opportunity to talk it out.

✓ Encourage group outings regularly, and don't expect your group to do this on their own time. Consider allowing one paid afternoon per month—as long as it's a team activity.

✓ Give employees time to talk. Managers are often so worried about work not getting done that they discourage personal conversations among their staff. What they don't seem to understand is that these conversations help employees feel connected to each other.

✓ Host informal breakfasts or lunches. Your department needs to make informal connections occasionally. In a semisocial atmosphere you can introduce a new project, get creative juices flowing, or just kick off a new month. One senior manager in a public relations firm gave $25 lunch "chits" to the 60 employees in his unit three times a year. There was only one instruction each time: "Take someone you don't know well to lunch, and learn more about them and the work they do." Smart linking!

Linking to the Team or Department

Strong relationships at work are key to retaining your people. Most of us want and need colleagues to think with, work with, and create with. Some surprising research reveals that coworker support is a key to retaining engineers. Yes, engineers—those folks whom we often stereotype as task oriented and almost antisocial. The study found that engineers depend on the workplace as a primary source of social relationships.[34] The same is true for many of your key employees.

Alas

The competition offered me a 10 percent salary increase, and I took it. My boss was blown away by my resignation. He thought I loved my job and had no idea that I could be enticed away. So what grabbed me?

Frankly, it was a combination of things. I felt no real connection to my workplace or the team. Maybe if we had spent a little more time together, or I had felt more a part of things there, I might have stayed. The company I'm joining operates primarily in teams. I'm hoping that will provide more of the interaction that I'm looking for. So the money was attractive, but the chance to be part of a team mattered even more.

—Engineer, aerospace firm

Most emerging workers want to be linked to a group of people with whom they enjoy working. In fact, for the newest generation entering the workforce, the number one question on their minds may be, Will I work with a team I like? This is so true that they will even leave together. We heard recently of 13 IT employees resigning as a group!

Work atmosphere is the main reason I stay. We have an amazing teamwork philosophy. In fact, it doesn't matter where in the country I am. I can stop at any retail dealership and say, "Hi, I'm a fuel service engineer," and I'm immediately welcomed. It feels great to be part of a family like that.

—Gas station owner

Linking to the Professional Community

Professional communities exist inside and outside the organization. On the outside, associations give people a chance to helicopter up from their own organization and learn what is happening elsewhere. How are other professionals handling similar problems and pressures? What unique approach worked in their culture?

The *nonlinker's* fear is that employees at a professional meeting might think the grass is greener elsewhere. What if they get job offers? What if their association interests pull them farther away from the job? All are possible. But all this is still possible *even if* you don't support their involvement. Encourage your employees to join outside professional associations.

Linking professionals within the organization is as important as helping them to build links outside the organization. Encourage your employees to build their networks by joining professional and social groups in your organization. Have you ever talked with your employees about these groups? Have you complimented someone who took a leadership role in one of them?

> *Managers at Hallmark Cards, Inc., practice linking inside their organization. They encourage all administrative staff to attend monthly lunch meetings of The Hallmark Chapter of the International Association of Administrative Professionals.*

Here are some things you might do to help support and build professional connections for your team:

TO DO . . .

✓ Offer paid memberships in professional associations as a reward for work well done.

✓ Set aside time at staff meetings for your team to report on conferences or events they attend.

✓ Offer to bring several of your people with you to your meetings.

✓ Offer to speak at one of their association meetings.

✓ Ask all who have memberships in associations to contribute their association newsletters or journals to a reading table. Devote some time at a staff meeting to discussing articles from one of these.

We know that you can't build these connections *for* your employees. But you can take steps to model and encourage connective possibilities for them.

Linking to the Local Community

Getting your employees involved in community service is another way to help them feel linked. For some, these activities are a major reason for choosing one organization over the next or staying with their present one. You can support these efforts. Better yet, build your own. Either way, promoting a cause within your department or company gives employees a sense of pride, promotes teamwork, fosters a bond among employees, and provides skill development as well. Companies have involved their employees in classrooms, community centers, and public housing projects. What better way to build relationships than to work on a meaningful project together?

TO DO . . .

✓ Investigate local projects, discuss at a staff meeting, and ask for volunteers.

✓ Ask employees to suggest projects and select one or two (or more) a year as a group.

✓ Invite several local volunteer groups to describe what they are doing in the community, and encourage your team to volunteer together.

✓ Invite another key department (great networking for your employees) to join with you on a local community project.

How Can You Teach Your Employees to Link?

A.J. left the organization, in part, because there was no link. You could prevent that by asking your employees whether any of the following sounds appealing:

TO DO . . .

Ask employees whether they would like any of the following:

✓ Get straight feedback
✓ Learn a specific skill
✓ Hear about opportunities
✓ Get information
✓ Get help with an idea
✓ Get a specific job
✓ Gain visibility
✓ Find new contacts

Then ask yourself who else—inside or beyond your organization—could meet each employee's needs. Link each employee to the person most able to fill his or her needs by looking for these skills:

see MENTOR

- *Nurturing.* Nurture your employees. And encourage them to build personal relationships with others in the organization. Once the friendships are in place, the nurturing follows.
- *Sponsoring.* Find someone who can help them gain visibility, perhaps even recommend them for a new job. While you can be a sponsor for your employee yourself, you may also want to direct the person to a colleague or senior team member who might offer something different.
- *Teaching.* As a manager, you cannot be the only teacher for your entire staff. Find someone who can help an employee learn a new skill. This may be a short-term teaching experience or a long-term, ongoing association.

see INFORMATION

- *Informing.* Find someone who has information about what's going on inside or outside the organization and is able to share it. Remember, some of your colleagues are closer to the power sources than you are, and other people have different connections from yours.

- **Advising.** Find a person who is in a position to give good advice, someone who has seen it, been there, done that. The more you can point out these good advice-givers, the better.[35]

Let Them in on the Secret of Reciprocity

The Latin expression *quid pro quo* means "something for something" or, in a more contemporary translation, "If you do something for me, I'll do something for you." If linking is only used to ask something of others, it will become one-sided and self-serving.

We often hear stories of "elegant currencies"—things you can offer that are easy for you to do that the other person needs but lacks resources to do. For example, you can teach somebody a new computer program. You can tell someone about a book you've read that could be invaluable to his or her work or even summarize it for him or her. There are a myriad of ways that people can offer something in return.

TO DO . . .

Quid Pro Quo Menu. Services you can offer to your "links" in return:[36]

✓ Introduce links to others (example: a potential client or supplier).
✓ Provide original ideas (example: a new way to process orders).
✓ Help others brainstorm (example: creative new ways to market a product).
✓ Volunteer help (example: at another's charitable event).
✓ Increase others' networks (example: provide names of contacts another needs).
✓ Reduce others' workloads (example: offer to help write part of a proposal).

✓ Offer feedback (example: suggest ways to improve the marketing brochure).

✓ Recommend to others (example: market product by word of mouth)

✓ Share expertise (example: computer skills).

And direct reciprocity doesn't have to be the only way this works. A hit movie based on the book *Pay It Forward* suggested that individuals offer to "give back" by giving to three other people. Eventually, we'd all win. Imagine an organization that holds this kind of philosophy and actually plays it out. Perhaps you could begin this in your own department. Ask your employees how they can "pay it forward" to colleagues, to their profession, to their community, to their organization, perhaps even to their industry.

BOTTOM LINE

Connections (great people, my team, my peers) are a major reason people say they stay with organizations. (Remember, it was number three on our list.) If links are weak or nonexistent, leaving is easier. In the constantly changing work environment, it is up to you to strengthen whatever bonds you can between the people who work for you and others in the organization. Today's knowledge workers need to link to others to get their jobs done. Their links will strengthen yours—in the perfect *quid pro quo*—and they'll be more likely to stay.

Chapter 13

 **M**ENTOR

Be One

I wish I'd had someone to warn me about some of the political ins and outs that were never written in any policy manual.

—A.J.

People with mentors are twice as likely to stay. Senior executives and human resource professionals know this. That's why mentoring programs have doubled in numbers in recent years across all organizations. Companies that want to retain high-performing women and minorities are investing in mentoring programs; some believe good mentoring will break the glass ceiling. Mentoring has become a way not only to transfer crucial skills and knowledge but to inspire loyalty in new employees and emerging leaders.

Companies are giving creative incentives to mentors, pairing mentors with new hires, and offering group mentoring and online mentoring to hasten their employees' development of management and technical skills.

But this book is not about structured mentoring programs that are put in place by HR professionals or requested by senior management. This is about the mentoring that *you* can do, from your position as a manager, now. And, it's not that complex. The more you act like a mentor to your direct reports, the less they think about leaving.

"Barely weeks into his new job as a nurse manager, Robert Cordo faced a supervisor's nightmare: how to fire a problem employee. 'I kept calling on Charlotte. She walked me through it," says Cordo, who at 29 was promoted earlier this year from staff nurse to nurse manager at Baptist Hospital in Miami and found himself the boss to former colleagues, nearly all female and many of whom are older and more experienced nurses. What helped him navigate potential pitfalls was his informal mentoring relationship with Charlotte Gibson, another nurse manager who has been with Baptist for 35 years. 'Even if you've been a nurse for a long time, when you step into management it's a new role,' says Gibson. 'You don't need a mentor to ask medical questions. You need to know how to swim in office politics.' She guided Cordo in how to deal with his difficult employee, making sure he documented steps he did to turn it around and followed hospital policy in the termination. 'It's the toughest thing you'll do,' she warned him. 'Have your ducks in a row.'"[37]

So What's a Mentor to Do?

Model	Be aware of your own role modeling, and point out others who are good role models for your people.
Encourage	Support your people in the risk-taking that is essential to their growth.
Nurture	Get to know your people's unique skills and capabilities. Work with them to do the most with their talents.
Teach **O**rganizational **R**eality	Tell it like it is. Help them avoid those organizational minefields that are never written about in any policy manual.

Coping Models and Masterful Models

A wonderful maxim buried deep in management literature suggests that people are more likely to trust "copers" than "masters." People who cope aren't always successful and don't always get it right the first time. People who master never seem to step off the path, and they always have it together. If you believe that your people need to see you as having the answers and making no mistakes, then this aspect of the mentoring process will be the most difficult for you.

A world-class lecturer on effective parenting asked a group of 200 parents, many of whom were older, what they thought was the one (highly researched) way to definitely raise self-esteem in children. Hands went up. No one hit the jackpot. The speaker said that the ability of the parent to say "I was wrong" had the greatest effect on the self-esteem of children. The speaker then asked the audience how many remember their parents ever uttering those words. Not many hands went up.

So our question is, how real can you afford to be? We think the answer is "pretty real." For example, let's say you were unable to hold to a predetermined agenda at an important meeting. Debriefing with an employee ("Here's what I think happened. Did you see how I was side-tracked by Max's question?") is a wonderful way of mentoring.

Modeling as a mentoring behavior means watching for opportunities to show how you've coped, giving permission to others to do the same.

Just-In-Time Encouragement

Encouragement truly is all in the eye of the perceiver. For example, an employee says, "He never encouraged me," while her manager says, "I encouraged her all the time." How can you encourage effectively?

Clearly, attention and retention go hand in hand. It's easier for those who *have* been encouraged.

Some managers encourage naturally, through casual conversations. Here's the easiest approach to offering encouragement, just in time. It consists of three steps:

1. *Recognize:* Notice something.
2. *Verbalize:* Say something.
3. *Mobilize:* Do something.[38]

Any of the three steps will encourage, but all three combined are much more powerful. For example: Liliana gives a beautifully designed flyer to her manager and says, "I've been doing some fiddling with that new graphics program and the laser printer."

see CAREERS

Recognize. Manager: "Hmm, looks great. I didn't know you like this kind of stuff." *(Good)*

Recognize and Verbalize. Manager: "This is really good. Is this something you'd like to do more of?" *(Better)*

Recognize, Verbalize, and Mobilize. Manager: "If you like this kind of work, why not let Marc in Graphics know, and while you're there, find out when he's offering his next graphics course." *(Best)*

Impromptu mentoring of this type is even more important if you have limited time to meet with employees. For many employees, these simple interactions will send a strong message that they matter.

Nurturing on the Run

Countless employees who have left their corporations say that their managers never stopped long enough to understand them or support them in their development.

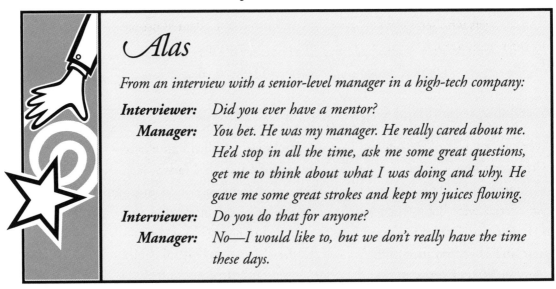

Alas

From an interview with a senior-level manager in a high-tech company:

Interviewer: *Did you ever have a mentor?*

Manager: *You bet. He was my manager. He really cared about me. He'd stop in all the time, ask me some great questions, get me to think about what I was doing and why. He gave me some great strokes and kept my juices flowing.*

Interviewer: *Do you do that for anyone?*

Manager: *No—I would like to, but we don't really have the time these days.*

Mentoring takes time—but not a lot. Mainly, it takes a willingness to show another person that you genuinely care.

Nurture Ideas. When employees come to you with suggestions or ideas about how they might approach something differently, do you immediately say no? Do you kill an idea before it is even off the tongue? (Tell the truth.) We hear that employees feel put down and turned down far more than their managers are aware. And that makes leaving easier. Instead, try listening to the entire idea, try playing with it as a "what if." Ask for more information. Sleep on it; mull it over. Think, "Isn't that interesting" *before* you think, "It will never work."

Nurture Relationships. Get to know your employees and give them every opportunity to get to know you.

> *A senior marketing vice president at a top-ten* Fortune *company commented that she wished managers in her organization would recognize how important a relationship with them was to their people. "And I don't mean anything deep," she said. "It's the little things, like a cup of coffee together once in a while." Employees want to feel they count and are noticed. When they feel invisible, it's easy for them to leave.*

Managers who seize every opportunity to nurture the talented people on their team are the managers who will keep those people.

Teach Organizational Reality

Everyone knows at least one sad story of a technically brilliant employee with everything to offer who derailed because of political blunders, lack of interpersonal skills, or ignorance of the unwritten rules. Countless corporate advice books suggest that academic brilliance alone does not make success. Daniel Goleman talks about EQ (emotional quotient—your ability to monitor your own and others' feelings).[39] Paul Stoltz refers to AQ (adversity quotient—your ability to deal with bad luck or plans gone wrong).[40] Others point to arrogance, insensitivity to others, or managing upward instead of down as career stoppers. Your ability and willingness to *tell it like it is* can save a career, perhaps for the benefit of your own organization.

Alas

She was technically brilliant. She graduated in the top 2 percent of her class in one of the top schools in the country. She was pursued by all of our competitors. We won. We offered opportunities for her to continue on her fast track, to work with other brilliant colleagues, to sit on a variety of committees that made decisions on our future direction. We had great plans for her.

She was so quick, though, that she started to rub people the wrong way. She continually ignored our chain of command. She stepped on toes. No one gave her any alternative ways to deal with the folks whose respect she needed.

Slowly, her influence eroded. Although she continued to be way out there in terms of what she knew, she just couldn't manage to communicate with her team or her peers. People avoided her. She became more and more isolated. And she became more and more unhappy with our organization. Before we knew enough to try to talk it out and give her some help, we lost her.

—Manager, high-tech company

How do you talk about unwritten rules? What if you coach someone about the buttons they press and you are wrong? Your view is just your view. Could you mess it up even more? We don't think so.

We have never heard of a manager who mentored too much and thereby lost an employee. We've never heard of a manager who coached too often and thereby lost someone's trust. We've never heard of a manager who talked too frequently about how he or she saw the organizational world and failed to retain talent for that reason.

Employees need to know your point of view. They want to know your take on how people get and give resources; what kinds of influence strategies work and don't work; and what certain senior leaders want and don't want in their reports, their presentations, and their meetings. And they want to know this before they walk into a minefield, or, at the very least, they want to be able to look at something that didn't work and understand why!

see TRUTH

> *A general manager in a worldwide chemical company participated in a group mentoring program. His responsibility was to meet with a group of high-potentials once a month for two hours and talk with them about whatever issues seemed important. He had one favorite question to put to each group, and he loved the dialogue that followed. He said, "I have a theory I call PIE. It's a success theory. Which part of the PIE do you think is most important? Performance? Image? Or Exposure?" He delighted in hearing the young brilliant chemical engineers all yell, "It's performance!"*
>
> *"No," he would say defiantly. "It is definitely not performance. We take that for granted. The greatest mark of success is Image and Exposure." The engineers hated that. They fought him every step of the way. They could not believe that this fluffy stuff could be so important, and it made them angry. But he stuck with it. He listened to their comments and acknowledged their rage. He explained that he felt that way too when he began in the company.*
>
> *Eventually, each group got it. And they appreciated him for raising the issue and teaching them that not-so-pleasant lesson. Whether all of them heeded his words we don't know. Those who did were probably more successful. But all appreciated the discussion and his candor. They never forgot it.*

So if you are nodding your head, consider using one of your own staff meetings to open a dialogue on organizational reality.

TO DO . . .

Invite your team to talk about any of the following topics:

✓ What have I learned about what counts in this organization?
✓ How have my failures and successes grown me?
✓ What most surprised me about the culture?
✓ What was the most difficult culture shift for me to make?
✓ What are the ways to get in really hot water here?
✓ How do people derail themselves?
✓ What do I know now that I wish I had known then?

People have a hunger for frank conversation in organizations today. Because of the intense competition, few employees feel that they can really express themselves or ask the questions that are on their minds. Most people claim they do not like playing politics. But because it's a reality of corporate life, a mentor watches out for the organizational well-being of a protégé. A mentor educates and protects a protégé from stumbling. A manager who is intent on keeping talent can adapt some of these principles.

Following a seminar, the authors received this letter from one of the participants:

My reason for writing is to share an anecdote about a mentor who made a difference in my career. He did so in many ways, but one relatively recent one stands out. We had spent weeks working together on the development plan for one of my stars. It took many calls, many lengthy discussions; there were many issues involved, but we worked with the star to design a plan that made sense.

But here's what stands out. When we finished the last discussion and agreed it would work, I looked at him and said "done." I remember slumping back in my chair and taking a deep, relief-filled breath.

I was happy we had settled things and happy that we were able to work out a solution. But in addition to that, I looked around my desk and saw all the pending projects, briefing papers, and other things that were piling up and had all taken a back seat to the week's ordeal. And what I said was, "Boy, I'm glad that's over. Now we can get back to work."

He locked my eyes and said, "You just don't understand, Joe; this is our work. If we don't do this, we have nothing. This is our job." And he found an empty spot on my desk amid the papers and pointed to it, adding, "This is what we do. Don't ever forget it."

Now there's a mentor.

One More Thing

Know one of the best ways of mentoring? Let your people mentor you. Let them tell you what they know. Ask them to tell you how they see the world. Let them coach you about how you might be more effective in *their* development. Observe. Stay open. You'll be amazed at how much you'll learn. And in the process of learning, you can't help but model, encourage, nurture, and teach organizational reality.

BOTTOM LINE

Your employees want you to teach them the ropes, and they know their careers will suffer if you don't. They want you to tell your own stories. Your failures and your success stories provide valuable insights that just don't come in other ways. Managers who share their experiences establish great rapport with their employees and find that there is a strong payback in engagement and retention.

Chapter 14

NUMBERS

Run Them

*My friend's boss told her that she could be easily replaced with some-
one who costs a lot less. He said it half-jokingly, but she knew that
there was a serious side to his statement. She left because she wants
to work for someone who values the work she does.*

—A.J.

Imagine that you arrive at work one morning to the evidence of a burglary. A brand new desktop computer has disappeared from an employee's desk. You call the building security office and the police. Then you launch your own investigation. You are determined to find out how this happened and who is responsible. You will not rest until the case is solved. And you immediately increase security measures—no more property will be lost.

Now think about the last time one of your most talented employees was stolen by the competition or just walked out your door. What kind of investigation did you launch? What measures were implemented to prevent it from happening again? Maybe the loss of a $40,000–$200,000 asset set off no alarm bells because no one ever really assessed the cost of losing talent. It doesn't take long to run the numbers. And you may be surprised.

Numbers and financial statements are the universal language of business. Frontline workers and senior managers alike understand them.

A major healthcare organization conservatively estimated "regrettable" turnover at $60 million in one year, while a Silicon Valley high-tech firm found their turnover costs to exceed $120 million per year.

*****

We're not just losing good people; we're losing great people. Almost one in every five of the people who leave us voluntarily every year is our top performer. The cost of this turnover in lost productivity, paperwork, recruitment, and training is huge—it's in the tens of millions of dollars.

—COO of a major bank

A careful assessment of the numbers might just convince you to focus more heavily on retaining your talent.

What's the Price Tag?

You may think these dedicated, talented people who have been critical to your success are easily replaced. And yes, you might even find replacements at lower salaries. We hear this argument often, especially during periods of high unemployment when many good people are looking for work. Often, though, the managers who say this have simply not calculated the real costs of turnover. Most experts agree that replacing a key person on your staff will cost you two times that person's annual compensation. "Platinum" workers (highly skilled professionals) could easily cost you four to five times their annual salaries.

Alas

John was one of our most talented engineers and was responsible for inventing some of our key technology. After a phenomenally successful year, he expected some kind of reward or recognition from his boss. When nothing was offered (not even a thank you), he met with his boss and

(continued)

128

asked for a 15 percent raise (about $15,000). His boss immediately said, "Forget it!" John did and left the organization to join a competitor who was thrilled to pay him 30 percent more than he had been making. Some said, "Oh well, we'll replace him within weeks."

Here's what actually happened:

✓ We hired a headhunter for $40,000 to try to steal someone like John from a competitor.

✓ After a three-month search, we found five good candidates and flew them all in for interviews at a total cost of $5,000.

✓ We selected the new guy (after much wining, dining, and selling) and agreed to a sign-on bonus of $10,000 and a moving allowance of $25,000. His salary was negotiated at 25 percent above John's ($20,000 difference in the first year).

So the bottom line in salary and expenses looked like about $100,000 to get the new guy in the door. But wait, that's not all.

✓ Our competitor won John (including his brilliant brain and technical knowledge) and went on to win a multibillion-dollar contract that would have been ours.

✓ John's buddies all started looking around, and the company executives got wind of it. Senior leadership decided to give them a 15 percent raise for two years in a row (at a cost of $200,000).

✓ We lost two or three other key people to competitors. Their technical expertise went with them. Our cutting-edge technology leaked out the doors, and we made our competition stronger almost overnight.

So it wasn't a $100,000 cost after all. It was literally billions. And this does not take into account the harder-to-measure costs of lowered morale, discontent, and lowered productivity following John's departure. In hindsight, it is clear that his boss (and others) should have worked a little harder to keep John. They should have recognized him, paid him what he was worth in the market, and also made certain that he was challenged and happy with his day-to-day work. Losing him was a very costly mistake.

—Manager, aerospace company

This true story may seem unusual. Certainly not every employee is worth billions to your bottom line. However, no one, other than the manager in this story, ran the numbers to figure out what losing John actually cost. Managers seldom do, because then they would have to look for the real causes of turnover or find somewhere to place blame. They might even need to create retention strategies. Most leaders just don't want to do all that.

Some readers have reacted to this story by saying, "Hey, wait a minute. John left for more money. We thought you said it's seldom about money!" Even in this story, his departure was not really about the money. It was about being heard, being appreciated, and being valued. John was hurt and frustrated by a boss who did not recognize or reward his efforts and who immediately dismissed his request for a raise. So what could John's boss have done differently? He could have

✓ Praised and thanked John for his major contributions.
✓ Listened to John's request and acknowledged that he was worth the raise—and that he would see what could be done and by when.
✓ Asked John what else he could do (if not an immediate raise) to reward him for his contributions.
✓ Calculated the cost of keeping John ($15,000) compared to the cost of losing him (you saw it—billions!).

see ASK

You will never really know what it costs to lose a talented employee if you never calculate the cost.

With the real cost of losing talent in mind, we recommend using the following table to assess the cost of replacing one of your excellent employees.[41] We have left blanks for you to add items that are relevant in your organization.

Item	Cost
Newspaper/Internet ads	_____
Search firm	_____

Item	Cost
Referral bonuses	_____
Interview costs: airlines, hotels, meals, etc.	_____
Employee's lost productivity prior to leaving (disengagement, resumé update, time on Monster.com job searching, time spent interviewing, negotiating and accepting new job)	_____
Manager's and team members' time spent interviewing	_____
Work put on hold until replacement is on board	_____
Overload on team, including overtime to get work done during selection and training of replacement	_____
Orientation and training time for replacement	_____
Lost customers	_____
Lost contracts or business	_____
Lowered morale and productivity, time spent talking about it around the water cooler	_____
Sign-on bonus and other perks	_____
Moving allowance	_____
Loss of other employees (They follow each other!)	_____
_____	_____
_____	_____
_____	_____
_____	_____

Notice that some of these costs are *direct,* such the cost of ads or sign-on bonuses, while others are *indirect,* such as overload on the team and lost customers or business (opportunity costs). Ironically, some of the indirect costs are the highest.

Alas

As part of a cost-cutting initiative, a boss told his department manager to let go of one of the department's four associates. The manager took some time to decide which person to cut, since they all had the same job responsibilities. Finally, he selected the poorest performer. But before he informed the unfortunate person, the best-performing, most experienced associate resigned. The manager was relieved because he was spared dismissing anyone. The manager's boss was pleased because the head count had been reduced. Yet the story's ending is anything but happy. The productivity of the person who resigned was nearly five times greater than the one who would have been laid off.[42]

In addition to running the numbers using the table, you might ponder these questions:

✓ How much money would your organization save if it reduced turnover by one percent?
✓ How would your organization use those dollars if they did not have to be spent on recruiting, hiring, and training new employees? (Consider employee development, enrichment programs, bonuses, incentives, or research and development.)

BOTTOM LINE

Retaining your best employees is a strictly rational business strategy. In business terms, you need to calculate the costs of losing and replacing key talent. For those who believe in the "easy come, easy go" philosophy of hiring and turnover, assessing these costs objectively can be eye-opening. Running the numbers can sharpen your commitment to keeping your most valuable employees.

Chapter 15

OPPORTUNITIES

Mine Them

I left for a better opportunity.

—A.J.

A. J.'s statement summarizes countless exit interview responses. Sometimes it's just the politically savvy thing to say (rather than saying, "My boss was a jerk"), and sometimes it's the truth. Talented people have many choices about where they work. To keep them, learn how to "opportunity mine" with them. Opportunity mining means looking for, finding, and then retrieving opportunities with your people. This does *not* mean that you are in charge of their career paths. It is not up to you to find their next exciting job. But if you really want to retain them, you must help them find opportunities on your own turf to compete with the ones they'll find elsewhere.

Alas

Lynne was a rising star, destined to do great things for the team—and her excellent work always made her supervisor look terrific. When she

(continued)

gave notice and her manager asked why, she answered, "I've been very happy here. You're a fantastic boss and the people are wonderful. It's just that I'm ready for something new, and this opportunity popped up in another company. I wasn't really looking for it; it just happened. I've decided to go for it."

The manager felt absolutely sick about losing her. What on earth would the team do? He offered more money, but the lure of this new, exciting opportunity had her already mentally and emotionally out the door. And when the manager probed a bit, he realized that the very opportunity she was leaving for was available within the department. Responsibility rests on both sides. She didn't ask, and her manager didn't offer to help her look for the next opportunity.

Avoid that scenario and keep your talent through a three-step process that we call "opportunity mining." Before you consider the three steps, consider your own views on opportunities at work.

Are You Opportunity High or Opportunity Shy?

To discover opportunities, one must look at the world in a new way, through a new lens. It is impossible to make people smarter, but you can help them see with new eyes.

—Gary Hamel, *Harvard Business Review*

Opportunity mining means opportunism in the most positive sense of the word. Its three key behaviors are *seeking, seeing,* and *seizing.* (The opposite of an opportunity miner is an opportunity whiner—you know, the one who is constantly complaining about his lot in life and at work.)

As a manager, you can partner with your employees to opportunity mine. Begin by getting a feel for your own level of opportunity mindedness. Complete the Opportunity Audit below to find out if you are *opportunity-high* or *opportunity-shy.*

OPPORTUNITY AUDIT [43]

Using the following scale, jot down the number that best indicates the extent to which each statement is true for you: 1 = rarely; 2 = sometimes; 3 = usually; 4 = always.

I am at ease when considering other people's viewpoints.   ____

I seek and use new technologies for improving productivity.   ____

I know the trends in the marketplace; I could tell you what competitors are doing and why.   ____

I take an active role in professional group(s).   ____

I network to help launch and support my career growth.   ____

I am flexible about adjusting plans when the first or second attempts at something fail.   ____

I am quite comfortable interpreting the "gray" areas of policy and practices.   ____

I let my career interests be known through formal (job posting) and informal (conversation) channels.   ____

I know how to connect people and information, and others seek my help in gaining access or information.   ____

How did you do? If you are opportunity high (scoring over 27), you are probably already seeking, seeing, and seizing opportunities for yourself and maybe even with and for your employees. If you scored on the low end (anything less than 18), you might benefit from the suggestions that follow. Only the opportunity-minded manager can truly help employees find possibilities for themselves.

There is no security on this earth; there is only opportunity.
—Douglas MacArthur[44]

OPPORTUNITIES
Mine Them

Seeking Opportunities

Too many employees and managers walk around their organizations not searching for opportunities. Or they seem to notice only the negative news or the black cloud on every bright horizon. People who seek opportunities, however, often see the glint of something new—and can follow through for themselves *and* for their people. Your willingness to seek will model this positive action for your employees. *It's important for you as well.*

Do you ever ask employees about the types of opportunities they might be looking for and even help them look? (Yes, even if it means some good folks leave the team.)

One engineering firm is an opportunity-rich organization where managers are opportunity seekers. They have developed a culture where employees feel comfortable speaking up when they are getting bored or need or want a new challenge, a promotion, or a different type of work. Managers hold regular employee development meetings to discuss their employees' interests and desires. They surface new possibilities and link employee goals with opportunities that already exist or are on the horizon. After several years, the results are measurable and positive. Not only do they retain their talented people, but they also have enhanced recruitment, as interviewees see the company as an opportunity-rich organization.

While this company launched their system-wide approach formally, it doesn't have to be done that way. You can do it yourself.

Hold development meetings with your employees. Your only topic should be their careers and what opportunities they might be seeking. "What if there are no opportunities here?" you ask. "What if I just open a can of worms by asking my employees what they are seeking? And what if I simply cannot help them, or by opening the conversation, I encourage them to leave?" To answer these tough questions, put yourself in their shoes. How do you feel about a boss who wants to help you seek opportunities for yourself? What happens to your level of respect and commitment while you work for him or her? What happens to your sense of loyalty to this boss and even to the team or company? It all goes *up!*

---

see ENRICH

TO DO . . .

✓ Ask your employees what opportunities they seek.
✓ Brainstorm with them to surface opportunities to enrich the jobs they currently hold.
✓ Check with managers in other departments to find out where new possibilities lie.

And remember: You won't see it 'til you seek it.

Seeing Opportunities

What does this say?

OPPORTUNITY
ISNOWHERE

✓ Opportunity is now here.
✓ Opportunity is nowhere.
✓ Opportunity I snow here. (You're in trouble if you picked this one.)

Most of us immediately lock on to one perspective and remain fairly confident in our findings. You may have chosen the first answer or the second and did not even consider the possibility that there is another point of view. Try this with your people. It is a great opener for a discussion of opportunities.

Just as you may have seen a phrase different from what your employee or colleague saw in the exercise, you may see plenty of opportunities in the organization while your talented employee sees none.

If you are an opportunity-minded manager, you will help your employees *seek* opportunities but will also help them to see those opportunities when they are right in front of their faces. You can shed the right light, point out the features and distinctions, and turn the opportunity around or upside down to make it more visible. Best yet, you will teach your employees how to do those things for themselves.

In partnership with your employees, ask, "Where and how carefully are we looking?"

A manufacturing company has an insiders' network of more than 360 people across the organization who are willing to take the time to talk with employees who want to learn about the nature of their work and the requirements of their jobs. This network has a computerized database (called Internal Information Interview Network) with the names and backgrounds of all the employees who participate.

Another organization we know of holds internal career fairs. The message to their talented people is that if they're looking for a new opportunity, they can look inside first!

What great ways to share information about opportunities. And what great ways to see if a pasture that looks greener really is greener. If your organization doesn't have databases or internal career fairs, you can still send folks who are wondering (and wandering) out to interview or e-mail people you know in other areas. Some managers let employees see by offering them the opportunity to fill in for others on vacation or sabbatical. Could you do this?

TO DO . . .

✓ Look around to see what is changing in your department, division, or organization. What new projects are on the horizon? What department is expanding; which one is shrinking? Who might be retiring soon or leaving for a new opportunity, opening up a possibility for one of your stars? Talk about these potential opportunities with your employees. Look carefully, and dig deeply for possible opportunities.

Seizing Opportunities

Many people are quite good at both seeking and seeing opportunities even when they are camouflaged. But many of us are not so good at the most critical behavior of the opportunity-minded person: seizing. For example, you may know someone who has a list of stocks or property she *almost* bought, a sport he *almost* learned, or a trip she *almost* took.

If you scored opportunity high on the Opportunity Audit, you probably seek, see, and seize quite well. If you want to retain your top talent, help them learn to seize opportunities that come their way. What are the barriers to seizing opportunities? It may be helpful to figure out why your employees fail to act, and what you might do to help them.

TO DO . . .

✓ If your employees do not create an action plan for their careers, help them analyze why they don't, and then help them do it. These plans should have action steps with time lines, potential obstacles, and support needed (what kind and by whom).

✓ If your employees do not adhere to their plans (too busy, resources delayed), you could help them. Suggest regular meetings to discuss progress, and brainstorm solutions to obstacles.

✓ If your employees second-guess themselves (analysis paralysis), you could help them avoid this. With their agreement, point out second-guessing behaviors that are more apt to be delay tactics than true assessment. Again, with permission, push for action when they have done enough analysis.

✓ If your employees decide a particular opportunity is just not for them, you could help them decide if it truly is not the right choice. After careful assessment, some opportunities are best passed by.

✓ If your employees let others talk them out of it, you could help them be strong in the face of naysayers and risk-averse "friends" and colleagues. Those people may be opportunity-shy (and sometimes even opportunity whiners).

✓ If your employees are just plain afraid to act, you could help them face the fear and just do it! Sometimes we just need an ally to provide support and courage when we get the jitters. Talk about the *what-ifs* with them—what if you try it and it doesn't work out? Usually the risks are not really life-threatening, even though they may feel like it.

He who refuses to embrace a unique opportunity loses the prize as surely as if he tried and failed.

—William James[45]

BOTTOM LINE

Our research shows that, more than any other single factor, people stay in an organization because of opportunities to be challenged, to do meaningful work, and to learn.

If you hope to keep your talent on your team, you must become opportunity minded—an *opportunist* in the positive sense of the word—on behalf of your people. If they come to you wanting something new or something more, partner with them to find opportunities. Be glad that you have ambitious opportunity miners on your team. Be forewarned, too. If you can't help them to seek, see, and seize opportunities at home, you will certainly lose them to organizations that can.

Chapter 16

Passion

Encourage It

The work was okay, but my heart wasn't in it.

—A.J.

Do you help your employees find the work they love to do? It may not always be easy, and you may even risk losing some of them. But if you don't partner with your talented employees to find work they are passionate about, you will no doubt lose them anyway.

Choose a job you love, and you'll never have to work a day in your life.

—Confucius

Passion for work means that people find what they do to be so exciting that it sometimes doesn't even feel like work—so exciting that it brings exhilaration, a "high." Granted, even those who have this passion seldom have it every day—but they do know that feeling, and they know when they lose it.

People Are Passionate

Do you know what your employees are passionate about? Do you have any idea what gets each of them up in the morning feeling anticipation and eagerness about the day? When we asked dozens of people about their work passions, here is some of what we heard:

- ✓ "I love creating something new, something no one has ever seen or even imagined before."
- ✓ "I get a kick out of working on such an elite team. There is so much brilliance here."
- ✓ "I love drawing, welding, building something."
- ✓ "I love numbers. I'd rather work with them than with people."
- ✓ "I really get excited when I discover a new rule in math."
- ✓ "I love to help someone get better at something and get happier in the process."
- ✓ "I love managing others. What a kick it is to motivate and guide a team to do great things."
- ✓ "My passion is turnaround—taking something that is broken and fixing it."

A common theme surfaces among these diverse answers: When people are doing what they love, they are at their best. If you help connect your employees' passions to their jobs, you and they will reap the rewards.

Passions are wired into the real world more directly than our work-day routines are. If you love something, you'll bring so much of yourself to it that it will create your future.
—Francis Ford Coppola

Uncover and Discover

So what can you do to help people find work that engages them deeply? First, ask. Ask several ways because people respond differently to different

see ASK

words. Try, "What work do you really love to do?" or "What are you passionate about?" or "What gives you the greatest thrill or kicks at work?" As they answer, dig a little deeper. Then think creatively about how you might put their passions to work.

A *Harvard Business Review* article described the efforts of Mark Levin, CEO of Millennium Pharmaceuticals, to keep the entrepreneurial spirit at his company alive.

> *"Each month, we all get together and brainstorm—the idea is to recreate the passion and fanaticism we had when everyone at Millennium could sit around one table. Each leader is responsible for communicating what we've discussed to his or her group and for kindling their enthusiasm, too. As a result, we have lots of small get-togethers at Millennium. All of this keeps the passion alive."[46]*

When was the last time you pulled your team together to ask for their ideas and to encourage them to build on one another's creativity? When did you sit down with one of your own team members and think together? Employees love the opportunity to think aloud with their managers; they want to "blue sky" occasionally. Do you know who wants this most? Who is most nourished by this kind of interaction? Have you made time for it? Have you made time for them?

When one manager had the "passion conversation" with his employee, here is how it went:

Manager: What do you love to do? What are you passionate about?

  Tara: I've recently learned to use some desktop publishing software, and I've created brochures for my church. I'm having a ball with it.

Manager: I wonder if there is a way we could use your talent and interest here at work.

  Tara: I've been thinking about it and wondered if I could take on the layout of the new company newsletter we've been talking about.

Manager:	How would that work out with your current heavy work-load?
Tara:	I will definitely get my work done. You know that about me. This project will be above and beyond my current workload.
Manager:	Let's give it a try. Keep me posted as you work on the first issue. Let me know what's working and what's not.

Tara was feeling pretty bored with her job. She'd been doing the same work for years, and the thrill was gone. She had even been thinking of leaving. She poured herself into the new project, teamed with colleagues, and turned out a first-rate newsletter. Her teammates and boss praised her and were astounded at her accomplishment.

Since that event, Tara has expanded her job to include multiple graphic arts projects. Her boss worked with her to restructure her job so that some of her former duties went to other people. Tara's energy and productivity have soared, and she wakes up eager to go to work. The key to her renewed enthusiasm is that her boss collaborated with her to uncover and then capitalize on her passion.

see ENRICH

What if passion lies outside of work? Some people are more passionate about skiing or about their children than about their work. What do you do then? Think about how the workplace might allow them to do more of what they love. Telecommuting, flextime, and on-site day-care centers are all strategies that support people's passions.

I can't imagine leaving this job. The day-to-day work is good and the team is great. But one of the best aspects of my job is that some of us go skiing most Fridays. We work hard all week to get the work done. We sometimes work evenings and even on the weekend when necessary. Then we take off. Skiing is my passion and this job allows me to enjoy it every week. How many of those jobs are there?
—Accountant, software company

This highly productive employee will continue to produce for his boss and team. That's the payback for his manager's flexibility.

TO DO . . .

✓ Ask your employees what they love to do. What are they passionate about?

✓ Dig deeper. Really understand what they are saying to you.

✓ Get creative. Collaborate with them to find ways to either
  • Incorporate their passion into the work they do
  • Flex the work somehow to allow time for their passion outside work

Passion Igniters

Most managers need a little help building passionate teams. Here are a few passion igniters to consider:

Hire for Passion

Why not select for passion in the first place? Find out if the candidate has a passion for making a difference or for your company's product or service. What about a passion for the work your unit does or for working on a team? If you build a team of passionate people, they'll not only produce for you—they'll actually help retain each other.

Show Your Passion

I see a world of possibilities where people who approach their work with passion, who take calculated risks for the good of the company, and who dare to test their own limits will reap unparalleled benefits in terms of excitement, fun, and personal satisfaction.
—J.P. Garnier, CEO, GlaxoSmithKline

What would it be like to work in an organization where leaders at all levels shared this CEO's approach? Share the passion you have for the work with your team. Your actions model what you expect from others.

Share a Meaningful Mission

Why does your team or organization exist? What is your mission? Share that mission with your employees. Then, clearly link employees' work to the mission. Tell them how their work contributes to it. Tell them how critical they are to you, to the mission of the team, and to the organization.

> *I've been the janitor and maintenance expert here for 30 years. We take care of old people who need nursing care and help with their daily living. They deserve the best, after all they have done and given in their lives. I love my work. I help make this building beautiful and safe for the people who work here and the people who live here. The director here gave me an award for my service and told everyone how critical I am to serving our residents. That award hangs on my wall at home.*
>
> —Maintenance expert, nursing home

This man is crystal-clear about the value of his work. He is inspired by the mission of the organization and the reason for his being there.

TO DO . . .

✓ Hire passionate people for your team.
✓ Share and show your passion for the work and for the people.
✓ Articulate and link people to the mission of your organization or team.

Passion Busters

Sometimes the fire is there, and it just plain goes out. People with passion can burn out if someone smothers their passion. There are two types of potential passion busters: one is the organization itself and the other, like it or not, is you!

Alas

He loved training and teaching others and told me he wanted to do more of that. Every chance he had, he would volunteer to teach a class, any class, even if it wasn't technical training. He learned to facilitate a team-building process that proved to be very successful in his business unit. But I just couldn't free him up to do more of what he loved. He was one of our best engineers, and we couldn't afford to have him pulled off his key projects to do this other work. How silly, in hindsight, that I was so protective of him and his time—now I have neither. He left us six months ago for a job that lets him utilize his talent and passion.

—Director, public utility

Organizational Constraints

Which organizational constraints prevent you from giving your employees different work or more of the kind of work they love? The list is often lengthy. Some people just call the constraints "reality." You might think that in reality we don't have enough of the following:

see QUESTION

- ✓ Time
- ✓ Money
- ✓ Staff
- ✓ Management support
- ✓ _____ (fill in the blank)

These constraints may be real. But remember, if you don't help your talented employees find work they love in your organization, you will lose them. Do you have enough time, money, and staff to deal with their loss and replacement?

Self-Interest

When you help your best employees uncover and pursue their passions, they may need to leave you to pursue those dreams. Out of self-interest (sometimes team interest), you might tend to avoid the passion discussion. Yet, your odds of keeping those people are better when you collaborate with them to find exciting, meaningful work right where they are.

> *My passion was the volunteer work I was doing in my community. My evenings and weekends were spent with a group that was working with inner-city kids in Los Angeles. We were mentoring them and providing safe playgrounds and educational opportunities. At work I honestly just showed up, did the minimum, and then shot out of there at 5:00 P.M. sharp. I sat down with my boss one day and described the volunteer work I was doing and how much it meant to me. He had a brilliant idea. He said that his boss had told him that the organization was committing to some new community outreach programs and that they were thinking of creating a new role in the organization. The next thing I knew, I became the director of community projects for our corporation. My work and my passion are now one and the same. As long as I can do this, I will never leave this organization!*
>
> —Director, entertainment company

The boss lost this employee from the team (it was inevitable)—but *saved* him for the organization.

TO DO . . .

✓ Assess the organizational constraints that serve as passion busters. Are they real? How can you overcome them?
✓ Be honest about your self-interests. Get clear about the costs and benefits of helping employees find work they love.
✓ Support and encourage your employees as they pursue their passion.

In the closing remarks of his book What Should I Do with My Life? *author Po Bronson tells the story of being invited by Michael Dell of Dell Computer to participate on a panel at a gathering of the Business Council, a group of over 100 CEOs from some of the biggest companies in the country. The panel was asked a great question: "What do employees want? What would it take to get more commitment out of them, more ideas out of them, more values out of them?"*

Bronson answered this way: "They want to find work they're passionate about. Offering benefits and incentives are mere compromises. Educating people is important but not enough—far too many of our most educated people are operating at quarter-speed, unsure of their place in the world, contributing too little to the productive engine of modern civilization, still feeling like observers, like they haven't come close to living up to their potential. Our guidance needs to be better. We need to encourage people to find their sweet spot. Productivity explodes when people love what they do."[47]

BOTTOM LINE

People who do what they love usually do it very well. If passion is missing at work, your best people may not bring their best *to* work. So collaborate with them to uncover and discover what they love to do. Link them and their work to your mission, and help them remove the barriers to doing what they love. You'll gain enthusiastic employees who will stay engaged and productive—and *on your team.*

Chapter 17

QUESTION

Reconsider the Rules

Twice in the last year I came up with some slightly unorthodox ways of approaching a problem. Each time I was told simply, "It would be against our rules to do it that way." I quit offering my ideas.

—A.J.

If innovation is so important, why is it so hard to support? Why is it so easy to say no before saying yes? Why is it easier to see if there is a precedent for what an employee wants to do?

When your employees come to you with new ideas, concepts, or rule breakers, they want to hear "You've got a point" or "Let's give it a try" or "Maybe that will work." They want to be recognized for their good ideas and innovative solutions, and they want *you* to support their questioning. You will increase the odds of keeping talented employees if you allow them to question the rules about their jobs, the workplace, and even the business.

A Rule's a Rule

The world would be even more chaotic if there were no rules. We count on rules to provide safety and sanity in our communities and workplaces. Yet most of us would agree that progress demands questioning the rules.

What if these people hadn't questioned the rules?

✓ *Wright Brothers:*   Why can't people fly?

✓ *Steve Jobs:*   Why can't everyone have their own computer?

✓ *Thomas Edison:*   Why can't we light our homes with electricity?

✓ *Fred Smith:*   Why can't we move packages across the globe over-night?

✓ *Jonas Salk:*   Why can't we prevent polio?

What if others hadn't asked these questions?

✓ Why can't we go to the moon?

✓ Why can't we reclaim Lake Erie to its former glory?

✓ Why can't we use lasers to perform surgery?

✓ Why can't we share data instantly over long distances?

✓ Why can't we build a computer after it's ordered?

✓ Why can't we create radar-invisible aircraft and ships?

You get the idea. The rule questioners and ultimately the rule breakers are our innovators. They improve our lives, and they are the backbone of successful organizations.

Alas

Darren was a new employee, hired to bring us fresh ideas and an outside perspective. He began to annoy us during his first month. He kept asking us questions like "Have you thought about doing it this way?" and "Why does this process take eight steps, when it could be four?" We held firmly to the way it had been done—why fix it if it ain't broken? Darren hung in there for six months and then shocked us all by leaving. He said that new ideas were not appreciated here. The sad thing is he's right.

        —Manager, medical technology firm

You might be thinking that Darren could have waited for a few months before suggesting all those changes. But didn't they hire him for his fresh ideas? Darren would have thrived in a workplace that truly encourages creativity.

So how open are you to the questions your employees bring you?

TO DO . . .

Complete the following sentences to determine whether you are more like Manager A or Manager B:

When employees ask me to question the rules, I most often

Manager A

❏ Give them a quick yes or no answer

❏ Give them the reasons why we do it this way

❏ Tell them I don't have time to deal with it

❏ Suggest they ask someone else

Manager B

❏ Tell them I would like to explore it further with them

❏ Avoid justifying how we currently do it

❏ Suggest a time frame for dealing with their question

❏ Collaborate with them to find other resources if necessary

If you are more like Manager A, you may be action oriented and highly productive. While you may have many excellent traits, you also could be a *question-unfriendly manager*. It won't take long for your employees to recognize that and

✓ Stop bringing you questions
✓ Shut down their creative, innovative brains
✓ Become less enthusiastic about work (and possibly less productive too)
✓ Leave you for a workplace where their questions are encouraged

If you are more like Manager B, you may also be highly productive. But you tend to respond eagerly and openly to your employees' questions, and you are a *question-friendly manager*. You are used to thinking, "What if that worked?" or "Why not see if we could change that policy?" or "How could this idea make us more productive?" You spend time brainstorming with your employees, and you collaborate with them to find answers to their questions.

Fifteen years ago (before flextime was popular), Barry went to his manager and asked if he could work a four-day week. He wanted to support his wife's growing business on the fifth day. That request was unusual and definitely represented a rule breaker, but Barry was a highly valued scientist, and his boss did not want to lose him. His boss considered the request carefully and worked to gain approval. It worked. Barry is still producing and innovating for that organization because his boss reconsidered the rules.

Think about the people who first asked about these policies:

✓ Job sharing
✓ Flextime
✓ Telecommuting
✓ Casual dress
✓ Self-managed teams
✓ Childcare centers
✓ Employee ownership plans
✓ Maternity/paternity leaves

These are just a few of the workplace innovations that many employees now take for granted. How would any of these ideas have been welcomed in your organization 15 years ago? How about today? If they are against the rules in your workplace, question the people who could change them.

A group of highly valued engineers from India had what some people heard as a couple of strange requests. They asked their manager to ask the senior engineering manager
✓ To put carpet in their work area so they could take their shoes off and line them up against the wall, according to their custom
✓ To install a small kitchen so their wives could come in to cook their preferred Indian cuisine

There was no precedent for this request, and the policy manual certainly didn't support it. The senior engineering manager considered

see SPACE

the cost ($5,000) and the gain (a very happy team), and said "Yes." He said it was the best $5,000 he's ever spent to motivate and retain a talented work group.

This team's manager had the courage to forward their request. And the senior manager had the foresight to listen, as well as the courage to act. Are you like these managers?

Please Hold Your Questions Until the End

How many times have you heard that? Usually there is no time for the questions. Or the speaker didn't really want questions. If you are a question-friendly manager, you welcome employee questions and innovative thoughts at any time, in any amount, and on any topic.

> *A question not asked is a door not opened.*
> —Marilee Adams, author *Change Your Questions, Change Your Life*

Imagine the talent that is lost (often to the competitor) because no one took the time to listen to the challenging questions of innovative people.

Alas

He was always too busy, and we knew we shouldn't bother him with questions or new ideas about our processes. He liked to work by the book, and he wanted us to follow the rules and just get it done. The sad thing was, our team came up with a better, faster way to turn out a superior product. We knew that if they were ever given a chance, our ideas could make money for the company. We kept our mouths shut and just kept working. I left the company and found a more innovative place to work.

—Supervisor, manufacturing team

Too Much of a Good Thing:
Rules, Guidelines, Policies, Procedures

All are necessary to some degree, especially to effectively operate large, complex organizations. But the rules often take on a life of their own. They multiply, they live in huge manuals, and they begin to stifle productivity and creativity. One team jokingly called themselves a "ship of rules."

Serena: Did you know that this approval form to spend $30 came back to me after three weeks in the organization with 15 signatures, including the CFO's?

Boss: Why on earth would it take all of that ridiculous time and effort?

Serena: It's the rule.

Boss: Let's see what we can do to break that one!

Reengineering (a process widely used in the 1990s) was all about tearing down those restrictive rules. Many organizations literally started with a blank sheet of paper and created brand new processes, usually with fewer rules and steps. One hospital pulled all its employees into a large meeting room to examine the way they were doing the work. They had a mock patient enter their system. She and her paperwork moved around the room and met with people representing admissions, diagnosis, referral, and treatment. Every stop represented the accepted rule and step for either the patient or her paperwork. The exercise revealed (to the horror of everyone) that one patient and her paperwork had made 50 stops through a bureaucratic maze before she began treatment.

Overgrown rules sometimes need questioning. If your talented employees get bogged down in them, they will spend too much time navigating the bureaucracy, not to mention filling out paperwork. They will spend too little time innovating and creating new solutions, services, or products. They will also look for an opportunity to work elsewhere, in a freer workplace with fewer rules and restrictions.

TO DO...

✓ Encourage your employees' questions. Let them know that any time is a good time to ask.

✓ Support your employees' attempts to reduce the number of rules in your organization.

✓ Hold regular rule-busting meetings just to look at rules, systems, and procedures that no longer work. Put different employees in charge of each meeting.

Are You Boxed In?

You have no doubt been asked (probably more than once) to think "outside the box." How ironic that most managers feel like the box has been handed to them (often by their bosses) and that they are supposed to think and act inside of it. An old training exercise (source unknown) suggests that the box typically feels fairly rigid, as if it were made up of concrete walls—the rules. But with a shift in thinking, your box can be composed of different materials, each with unique properties. Here is an example:

This box has walls made of four materials.

✓ **Concrete.** This wall represents rules that are truly rigid. It cannot be broken, pushed, bent, or shattered. *"You must have a medical degree to practice medicine in this hospital."*

✓ **Glass.** This wall is strong and sturdy, but if you hit it just the right way with just the right instrument at the right time, it will break. It represents the rules that may seem unbreakable but actually can be broken. *"Women will never be Supreme Court justices."*

✓ **Rubber.** This wall is thick and strong, but it has some give to it if you are willing to push hard. It represents rules that might be pliable. *"We all put in a 40-hour week, from eight to five, five days a week."*

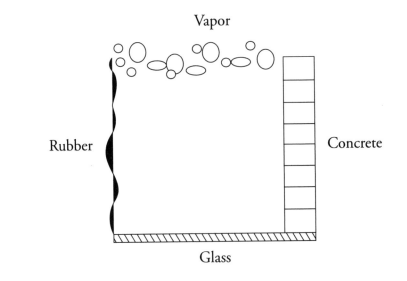

✓ **Vapor.** This wall is made up of our beliefs, assumptions, and perceptions about the rules. *"People will never fly."*

If you examine the rules you operate by, you will find that few of them are truly concrete. They just feel that way. The most formidable aspect of the box is often the vapor wall. Your beliefs and assumptions—or the company's—often prevent you from questioning the rules. They may also keep you from hearing your employees' questions.

SportsMind is an organization that specializes in experiential learning and high-performance team building for managers. One exercise in a week-long training session is to climb a 30-foot pole and leap off the top to catch a trapeze (supported by safety lines, of course). One group included a paraplegic manager in a wheelchair who wanted very much to take part in all the activities. Many in the group had a vapor wall of beliefs and assumptions that said he could not be part of the pole exercise. But he insisted, the trainers huddled, and between them they found a solution. He climbed the pole, using the strength of his arms and the support of safety lines while his team shouted from below. When he reached the top he cried—and so did we.

—Former trainer with SportsMind

That participant and the trainers who worked with him found a way around the vapor. When it was over, he said that he would never again feel constrained by the rules.

TO DO . . .

✓ The next time your employees question you about the rules (about their jobs, the organization, or the work at hand), stop before you say, "It can't be done."

✓ Check to see which wall is holding you (and others?) in the box.

✓ Unless it is truly the concrete wall, work with your employees to bend or break the rules. Test the vapor wall and the beliefs that box you in. Evaluate new ideas fairly before you discard them.

Question Yourself, Too

Not only do you need to be able to ask good questions of others, the best managers we know are able to also ask good questions of themselves. They are able to step back and question actions they have taken, and even consider actions they haven't taken. Their continual self-examination catches on with their employees. Here are some questions you might try, from Marilee Adams's book *Change Your Questions, Change Your Life*:

✓ What happened?

✓ What's useful about this?

✓ What do I want?

✓ What can I learn?

✓ What is the other person thinking, feeling, needing and wanting?

✓ How can this be a win-win?

✓ What's possible?

✓   What are my choices?

✓   What is best to do now?[48]

BOTTOM LINE

How long has it been since you have questioned the rules? And how much do you encourage questioning? Allow your employees to ask about the way work gets done and about the rules that hinder their productivity and satisfaction. Support their questioning, and bend or break the rules to help them get what they need. You will greatly increase the odds of keeping your talent.

Chapter 18

REWARD

Provide Recognition

It wasn't about the money, really. Oh, sure, a bonus would have been nice when I brought that new client in or when I finished those specs ahead of schedule. But a "thank you—I noticed" would really have been appreciated.

—A.J.

So this is the chapter about money, right? If not, where is that chapter? Isn't money a major motivator and a key reason people stay in their jobs?

Our competitors all pay 10 to 20 percent more for identical work. They come after us year after year, trying to steal us away from our organization. A few of us have been enticed away. While I would definitely appreciate a raise, I would not leave just to get one. The reason is that I feel rewarded in many other, less tangible ways. I'm rewarded by the actual work I do and by the appreciation my boss always shows. He has told me many times how critical I am to the success of the team. He is caring and finds creative ways to recognize our efforts. I feel important and valued.

—Supervisor, entertainment company

Decades of research and common sense tell you to pay fairly or your best people might leave. Benchmark similar organizations in your industry and find out what the pay scales, bonuses, and perks look like. If you find that your compensation system is not competitive with that of similar companies, be concerned. Take your findings to your boss or to the compensation expert in your company and try to get things changed.

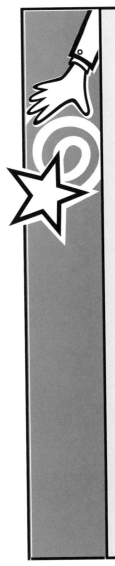

Alas

To: Executive Committee and HR

Working at TGP has been a wonderful experience. I accepted the challenge because of all the rumors in the travel industry that e-tickets and supposed fees would more or less eliminate our jobs as travel agents. I wanted to be well-rounded and marketable, and computers seemed to be the way to achieve this. Right away, I was able to learn Windows 95, Outlook, Word, Excel, and PowerPoint, which I would never have had the opportunity to do in a travel office.

I also enjoyed working with my many internal clients. It was a challenge at first, gaining everyone's trust, but gradually I was able to make headway and make the travel department a success.

Because of my decision to move to New Jersey and buy a house, I started to see what jobs were being offered and the salaries they commanded. I realized that my salary now was under market value for a ten-year agent. It seemed as though TGP and I were working this out, but unfortunately, that was not the case.

As of July 12th, I have accepted another position. I will be an official travel agent again, with my IATA card, incentives, and market-value salary. They will also be implementing a brand new state-of-the-art reservation system, which will keep me up to date on the latest

(continued)

computer technology. I will do my best to have everything cleaned up before I leave.

—Travel administrator

P.S.: In a note sent to the authors, her manager remarks:

This speaks volumes to what keeps people, and it also provides an underlying premise: you have to keep compensation competitive, or they'll find a place that will. This person was a gem to work with. I fought for her salary increase (which would have raised her salary by $3,000), but the executives refused to be "extorted." I did what I could. Now it will cost us much more than that to find her replacement.

Pay fairly and *pay competitively. But don't stop there.* The research that suggests you need to pay fairly to keep your people also says that money alone won't keep them on your team. It is not the major motivator. Challenge, growth opportunities, flexibility, great coworkers, meaningful work, a good boss, and recognition (often in nonmonetary forms) are examples of things that matter more to most of your people. When those are missing, talented people walk.

see ASK

A study called Rewards at Work[49] investigated how U.S. workers felt about the rewards they receive at work. The research examined attitudes toward five reward categories, including direct financial (pay), indirect financial (benefits), work content (the work itself), careers (long-term opportunities for development), and affiliation (feelings of belonging). The surprising finding in the study (though not to us) was that all five types of rewards were considered equally important.

A Word about Perks

During the talent wars of recent years, we've seen the proliferation of perks in the workplace. Employers have tried everything from volleyball courts to BMW giveaways to concierge services in an attempt to improve work life and/or to retain talent. While they may have worked to recruit some people, and they are often received happily by the workforce, no evidence exists that perks will help you hang on to your stars. It makes sense that if highly marketable employees are bored, don't like the boss, or see no career future with you, a massage on Friday afternoons won't keep them.

So focus on rewards that really work and are within your control.

Rewarding Rules

Rule #1: *If an employee expects it, it may no longer be viewed as a reward.*

Alas

Every year I received a bonus, some stock options, and a raise. I was hitting all the targets and doing a good job. It's funny how I left every one of those annual reviews feeling empty. The reward I wanted most was positive feedback from my boss. I wanted him to say that he really appreciated me and my contributions to the business. I really never felt recognized. That was a primary reason I left the company for another job.

—Manager, automobile manufacturer

You may think that the annual incentive bonus is ample reward for work well done. Your employee may see it differently. Many employees now expect bonuses, company cars, cell phones, financial planning services, and great healthcare plans as part of the package. They are no longer useful as special reward or recognition tools.

Rule #2: *Rewards need to match your employees' needs and wants.* How would you like to be recognized? We asked dozens of people this question. The following list represents some of what we heard. Notice the differences.

TO DO . . .

Check which forms of recognition, other than money, you might appreciate. Also note which ones might *not* matter to you. All of these are requests employees have made to their managers.

- ❐ An award, preferably given in front of my peers
- ❐ A plaque to hang on my wall
- ❐ A thank you, in writing, from my boss
- ❐ A note to my boss's boss about my excellent performance
- ❐ Frequent pats on the back
- ❐ My boss actually implementing one of my ideas
- ❐ A chance to be on a really exciting, cutting-edge project
- ❐ A day off
- ❐ Words of praise in front of my family
- ❐ A chance to go to lunch with senior management
- ❐ An opportunity to work with people from other parts of the company
- ❐ A chance to be on one of the important steering committees
- ❐ A promotion
- ❐ A change in my title
- ❐ A small memento or gift
- ❐ Some flexibility in my schedule
- ❐ More freedom or autonomy
- ❐ A seminar or training class

Many managers wrongly assume that everyone likes or wants the same types of rewards and recognition.

I will never forget the thrill of receiving an Excellence Award at the annual company conference. Seven hundred of my peers were there. My name was called and written in huge letters across a massive screen. As I walked forward, it truly felt like an Academy Award moment—almost surreal. There was a cash prize that accompanied a beautiful glass trophy with my name inscribed on it. I had my picture taken with senior management.

The cash was spent within weeks. But the trophy still sits on my desk, and the memory of that amazing moment of recognition will last a lifetime. I have never felt more appreciated or rewarded.

—Vice president, major consulting firm

see ASK

While this person was fully rewarded by all the hoopla at the conference, someone else might have been embarrassed or would have much preferred some other form of recognition. *Ask your employees what kind of recognition or reward they most appreciate.*

The Universal Reward

Compensation is a right; recognition is a gift.
—Rosabeth Moss Kanter, author and management consultant

Check your files. Somewhere in there is a letter from a boss thanking you for a job well done, right? You've cleaned out all the others over the years, but this letter of praise remains. Why is that? Praise works for everyone. There's really no such thing as too much praise (as long as it's sincere). Regardless of individual differences, virtually all employees want to hear how valuable they are to the team, how important their work is, and what great work they have done. And they are happy to hear it again and again.

Ken Blanchard's famous book, *The One Minute Manager,* reminds managers to praise their employees.[50] And in a study in *Incentive* Magazine, 57 percent of respondents indicated that they preferred to be recognized by an immediate supervisor, compared to only 21 percent who placed higher value on a presentation from the company president.[51]

We suggest you take your employees' individual preferences into account and then do the following:

TO DO . . .

Praise your employees in the following ways:

✓ *Spontaneously.* Catch people doing something right and thank them then and there. (Thank you, Ken Blanchard.) Leave voice-mail recognition messages. And that takes less than one minute.

✓ *Specifically.* Praise people for specific (rather than generic) accomplishments or efforts. See "Ten Sentences That Will Help You Retain Your Best Employees" (below).

✓ *Purposefully.* Take an employee to lunch or dinner at a great restaurant to show your appreciation of work well done.

✓ *Privately.* Go to your employee's office to give a personal thank-you and praise. (*Verbal* thank-you's are critical.)

✓ *Publicly.* Praise an employee in the presence of others (peers, family members, your boss). One team adds "shameless bragging" as a short agenda item in all staff meetings.

✓ *In writing.* Send a letter, memo, or e-mail. Possibly send a copy to team members or higher-level management. Don't forget—*written* thank-you's are a coveted workplace incentive.

Ten Sentences That Will Help You Retain Your Best Employees

The HR team at a major bank sent out a memo with recommendations to help managers make their praise more specific. They suggested that telling people "You're doing a great job" isn't going to make them want to stay. Praise can help you retain your top employees—but only if it is detailed and relevant. Here are the "openers" they recommended. Try using any of them with your own employees:

✓ *"You really made a difference by . . ."*
✓ *"I'm impressed with . . ."*
✓ *"You got my attention with . . ."*

✓ *"You're doing top quality work on ..."*

✓ *"You're right on the mark with ..."*

✓ *"One of the things I enjoy most about you is ..."*

✓ *"You can be proud of yourself for ..."*

✓ *"We couldn't have done it without your ..."*

✓ *"What an effective way to ..."*

✓ *"You've made my day because of ..."*

So many otherwise able managers act as if compliments come out of their bank accounts.

—Warren Bennis, author/consultant

Get Creative

As you struggle to think of other ways to reward and recognize your employees, try this. Think about yourself. What could your boss do that would really demonstrate how much he or she values you (besides giving you a raise or praise)? Remembering individual differences, you can use your own list to think about how to reward your employees. Here are a few hints that will get you started.

Time

What a precious commodity. Give an outstanding employee the afternoon off. Let another sleep late. Thank a whole team by giving them a Friday off. Let them decide when to use their gift of time.

> *One boss created a days-off bank. He put 25 days in the bank and then used those days to reward individuals and teams for outstanding performance.*

Toys

What toys might they want? A cappuccino machine? A dart board in the lounge? A volleyball court between buildings? Tickets to the movies?

Alan was so proud. He completed a set of last-minute specifications, stayed late, and in general went above and beyond. To thank him, his boss gave him a $150 check and told him to spend it on a "toy." Alan bought one of those miniature airball tables and proudly brought it home. His kids were excited, and when they asked why the gift, he answered, "It's not a gift for you. It's for me, from my company, for doing a great job." The kids were impressed. Four years later the toy is still in use in the family room. When anyone says to his kids, "How cool," they say, "Our dad got it for his good work." Alan smiles every time.

Trophies and Trinkets

What small memento or trophy would be meaningful? It could be a customized plaque, a coffee cup inscribed with a personal thank-you note, or a refrigerator magnet with the perfect message.

> *Simple observation suggests that most of us are trinket freaks—if they represent a genuine thanks for a genuine assist.*
> —Tom Peters, author and management consultant

*****

The Gumby award became treasured. It all started when one employee showed phenomenal flexibility in helping teammates deliver a project on time. He showed up at work the next day to find a giant Gumby doll sitting in his chair. It probably cost five dollars, but that trophy became the most sought-after prize in the organization and people were elated when it showed up in their offices.
                            —Consultant, transition consulting firm

Fun

Would your employees like taking an outing on company time? Leaving work early to play ball or to take a hike together? Playing hooky together and going to a movie? Having a spontaneous pizza party in the office some afternoon?

see KICKS

The team had been working long hours and even weekends. The boss suggested that we rent a limousine, buy some great food and wine,

and go to an outdoor concert. He picked up the tab. We felt so pam-
pered and rewarded for all the effort and our outstanding results.
— Vice president, compensation firm

Freedom

see SPACE

What kind of freedom might they want? Flextime? Freedom to work from home, to dress casually, to change the way they do some of the work? Freedom to work without supervision? Freedom to manage a budget?

One manager rewarded his secretary by giving her a monthly budget
of $400 to use as she saw fit. She could use her judgment to buy office
supplies, order lunch for the department, or something else. It showed
that her boss appreciated and trusted her.

Food

Some of the most popular low-cost rewards are food. One manager we know asks all new hires what their favorite candy is and then delivers that candy to them on their six-month anniversary. (Bev loves Chuckles; Sharon loves peanut M&Ms.) And people love gift certificates for dinner at a great restaurant. (Dinner for two is wonderful—dinner for the family is fantastic!) Use your imagination and find out what your team would really enjoy.

"It was one of those grunt jobs that employees in any organization
might have to do: move a computer center to a new location. Except
mortgage lender Fannie Mae asked more than 550 employees to do
their "day jobs" all week and then throw themselves into this new
task over 13 consecutive weekends, pulling all-nighters on Friday
evenings—without even a promise of extra pay."

"How? 'Napoleon said that an army marches on its stomach, and
I fed the hell out of these guys," says Mary Cadagin, the Fannie Mae
leader who spearheaded the move last summer. She's half-joking, of
course, but she did serve about 1,600 pounds of chicken wings to
her crews for midnight snacking—not to mention the Friday night
themed dinners, ranging from New England clambakes to down-

*home southern cooking, or the full-blown Saturday morning break-
fasts with pancakes, eggs, bacon and sausage."*

—John Byrne[52]

Small Money

Sometimes it's a small sum ($50–$100) to put toward whatever the rewarded employee wants. This discretionary, on-the-spot cash award is
sometimes more deeply appreciated than one might ever guess.

> *"This year the company my husband works for, after more than 20
> years, disbanded their holiday tradition of giving each employee
> either a turkey or ham at Christmas. Many employees were devas-
> tated, most were disappointed, and there was much grumbling. Eric
> and several of his management colleagues got together and gave each
> family in their "pyramids" a gift certificate to Kroger Grocery Stores,
> in a quiet show of thanks, and understanding of the hardship. That
> gesture went a very long way in saying thanks, happy holidays, and
> you're important to us. Doesn't excuse the parent corporation, but
> does help in the recognition and thanks arena!"*

—Leslie Barnes Carson

*****

*One internal marketing group in a medium-sized manufacturing
company decided to reward people they worked with each month. They
set aside $1,200 so that they could present a $100 gift certificate to a
person in the organization (from any other department) who had
worked with them, had helped them in some way, and was appreciated. The recipient was selected by the entire marketing team, and
each month one person surprised the recipient by presenting—the
gift at a most unexpected time. The idea was well received by all. The
marketing department enjoyed the process, and it was "small money."*

Big Money

Peter Cappelli, of the Wharton School of Business, says that higher wages
are not necessarily the principal way to lure good workers any more. Yet

it may be exactly what some people want. Find out which of your talented employees is truly motivated by money. See what you can do for them. Would a bonus for exceeding goals and expectations help? How about a larger raise than expected? Think about where you can stretch your budget to reward with money when it is warranted and *desired*. Remember it will usually cost you more to replace a star than to meet their salary requests.

If you think your hands are tied because more dollars are an impossibility, try this: Tell the truth. Then ask what else your employee might want. At first this may be uncomfortable for both of you. If you are patient, however, other alternatives will appear. You will discover at least one thing your talented employee wants that you can give. The key is that you let employees know how much you value them and their contributions.

TO DO . . .

Since the first edition of *Love 'Em or Lose 'Em*, dozens of managers have sent us their "creative reward" ideas. Check those you might want to try with your talented people:

☐ **The Golden Genie**—*I got these great wind-up toys from McDonald's—little genies that walk around. When someone deserves a pat on the back, I put the genie on their desk and let it walk around. Then I grant them any nonmonetary wish they have. I'm amazed; so far there has been nothing I have been unable to grant.*

☐ **Personalize the Paychecks**—*I have a small unit reporting to me. I write a personal note every two-week period, and it goes with their paychecks. Every two weeks, it forces me to think about something I noticed and appreciated. I've gotten great feedback on that.*

☐ **The Dream Gift**—*I had the opportunity to give a gift of a few thousand dollars to a key (gold-star) employee. Instead of giving the gift, I took the time to learn more about her, what she liked doing outside of* work. I learned (to my amazement) that she was an avid kayaker. I shopped for a kayak with several people on my team, and we brought it to work and presented it to her. Granted, you can't do this all the time, but if you could have seen the look on her face!

☐ **The Silver Snoopy**—*Johnson Space Center (NASA) gives 20 silver Snoopy pins out to employees who have made a big difference to the organization. The silver Snoopy has actually flown in space, so it is a highly valued gift.*

☐ **A Great Idea**—*I give out a lightbulb filled with candy to anyone who comes up with a great idea and brings it to me. I generate excitement that says "keep those ideas coming." I give several a month. People actually try to save the candy because they like leaving the light bulb on their desks.*

☐ **Never Missing a Beat**—*My organization gives out monetary awards for folks who aren't absent. One employee recently got one—he worked 23 years and never missed a day. The annual monetary award is for the number of years worked without absence. I started doing that in my own department on a much smaller scale, and it works just as well.*

☐ **Be the Best**—*Once a quarter I ask my team to submit someone else's accomplishment that impressed them. I read over all the accomplishments and give a day off to the award winner. It gives me a chance to see accomplishments I never even knew about, and it gives everyone a chance to recognize their teammates.*

☐ **Wall of Fame**—*I work in a customer service center, and I maintain our "wall of fame." Every time any of my people gets a letter from a customer about their service, it gets framed and put up on the wall. I also give the employee a small gift certificate. I think, though, that their "framed" letter means more than the gift certificate. Visitors love to read the letters. Does great for our internal PR as well.*

☐ **Treasure Chest**—*I keep a slew of low-cost items in a big box in my office. I call it the Treasure Chest—things like movie coupons, boxes of special candy, and restaurant vouchers. When I want to thank someone, I walk over to them, tell them what it is I appreciate, and invite them to select something from the chest. Yeah, it's hokey, but I am still surprised by how much they love it.*

❐ *A Good Thing to Remember*—*I try to remember that people—good, intelligent, capable people—may actually need day-to-day praise and thanks for the job they do. I try to remember to get up out of my chair, turn off my computer, go sit or stand next to them, and see what they're doing. I ask about the challenges, find out if they need additional help, and offer that help when possible. Most of all, I tell them in all honesty that what they are doing is important, to me, to the company, and to our customers.*

BOTTOM LINE

Over and over, research has told us that money is not the major key to keeping good people. We double-checked this research with our own, and it proved true. When employees across the country answered the question, What kept you? few had dollars in their top three reasons. People want recognition for work well done. Assess your pay scale to be sure it's fair. Then *praise your good people*. Find creative ways to show your appreciation, and you will increase the odds of keeping them.

Chapter 19

SPACE

Give It

My boss gave me no space to think or create or even manage my own time. I felt controlled and hemmed in with no room to grow.

—A.J.

Anyone who has raised a teenager (or remembers being one) knows the phrase *give me some space!* Someone who feels fenced in, overcontrolled, or frustrated by his lack of power over his own situation usually says it. Dilbert, the cartoon spokesperson for corporate American office workers, constantly profiles managers as control freaks who give their employees little or no space, either physically (cubicles) or figuratively (space to control one's own day-to-day existence).

Think about the last boss you had who dictated your every move, held stringently to the policy manual, or was never open to new ways of doing anything. How long did you stay in that job? (We hope you are not there now!) That boss didn't understand inner space or outer space. Employees will leave if they don't have enough of both.

Inner and Outer Space

By *inner space,* we mean the mental and emotional space your employees want and need to feel like creative, productive members of the team.

It includes space to

✓ Be self-directed
✓ Manage one's own time
✓ Work and think in new ways

As a manager, you can give your talented employees the inner space they want and increase the odds that they will stay on your team. (It usually costs you nothing.)

Outer space refers to the physical world and primarily to employees' work environment. It includes space to

✓ Design one's own work area
✓ Work from different places
✓ Take a break
✓ Dress as one wishes

see QUESTION

Managing your employees' outer space requests might require some boundary-pushing behaviors for you, especially if your organization has never done it that way. Before we tell you what some other managers are doing to give more space, take this short quiz to determine your own space-giving tendencies. Keep score.

TO DO...

Read the following scenarios, imagining that you are the boss of this team. Decide when you would say "Sure," "No way," or "Let me see what I can do." Use the answer box that follows.

1. For personal reasons, I want to come in half an hour earlier and leave half an hour earlier three days a week.
2. I want to get this task done in a brand-new way, not like you have seen it done before.
3. I want to complete the first five steps of this project before I have you review it with me.

4. I want to try a new technique, one that I am more comfortable with, to increase sales.

5. Instead of taking that class you recommended, I found a mentor to teach me that skill.

6. I just took some great pictures on my vacation and want to put them on my office/cubicle walls.

7. I want to work from home two days a week.

8. I plan to work on Saturdays for a few weeks in order to get a project done on time. I want to bring my well-trained dog to work with me on those days.

9. I want to wear casual clothes to work, rather than a business suit. I am much more comfortable and creative in my jeans and tennis shoes.

10. I know we've always done these projects solo, but I want to put together a team this time because I believe we will do the job better and more quickly.

11. I want six weeks off work (without pay) to begin building my own home.

12. I want to bring my new baby to work for the first six weeks of her life.

Answer Box

Your Response	1	2	3	4	5	6	7	8	9	10	11	12
Sure, no problem.												
No way.												
Let me see what I can do.												

The list of requests you just considered will give you a clue about the kind of space-giving we are talking about. The first five have more to do with inner space, and the remaining seven relate to outer space.

1. Count the number of scenarios where you said, "Sure, no problem, as long as you get the job done."
2. Now count the number where you said, "No way," "It's never been done that way," or "Our policy manual forbids that."
3. Finally, count the number of times you said, "Let me see what I can do for you," "I will need to take this to my boss," or "Tell me more about what you need, and I'll see what I can do."

How Did You Score?

"Sure, no problem."	8 or higher	You are *space-friendly*. Keep doing what works!
"No way."	3 or more	You are *space-unfriendly*. Try the "let me see" response next time!
"Let me see what I can do."	Any number	You are *space aware*. Your employees will appreciate your efforts!

In some organizations, every one of these requests would receive a positive response. But the opposite is true in far too many. Would you be surprised to know that those organizations are not on anyone's preferred employer list and that they are having greater difficulty recruiting and retaining their employees? We believe that no matter how well these organizations pay, they will ultimately lose their talented people, simply because they do not give them *space!* So how can you give employees the space they need?

Giving Outer Space

Space to Work from Different Places

One of the most frequent accommodations of space needs is allowing telecommuting. An article in *CFO* (chief financial officer) magazine stated:

"Not everyone agrees on just what constitutes a teleworker. The International Telework Association & Council defines one as an employee who works at home, at a client's office, in a satellite office,

a telework center, or on the road at least one day per month. Even restricting the definition to an employee who works from home at least one day a month, there are 23.5 million teleworkers in the United States. Most corporations with large numbers of teleworkers report productivity increases, not declines. 'A number of companies fear their workers will be at home with their feet up in front of the TV, and that's just not the case.'"[53]

Nancy Kurland, assistant professor of management and organizations at The University of Southern California's Marshall School of Business, said, "Telecommuters tend to work longer hours because they feel telecommuting is a privilege and they want to make sure it's not taken away."[54]

What if your organization does not allow it?

My company had never allowed telecommuting, and I believed it probably never would. One of my top employees asked me if she could work from home two days a week, and my immediate response was no. A month later she sadly handed in her resignation and said she had found an employer who would allow her to telecommute. I simply could not afford to lose her, so I went to my boss and asked if we might bend the rules on a trial basis, offer her telecommuting two days a week, and see how productive she was. She stayed with us, increased her actual productivity by 10 percent and is a grateful, loyal employee. Since then we have loosened our policy substantially and consider telecommuting on a case-by-case basis for any employee who requests it.

—Accounting manager, city government

This manager not only bent the rules (probably after reading the chapter Q) but also realized the importance of space.

Telecommuting is not an option for jobs that simply must be performed at the work site. If that is the case, think about other ways that you can give your employees space.

Sometimes the organization has no rule about working from another place, but the manager says no anyway. If you are one of those managers,

Alas

I think of myself as cutting-edge in many ways. But in other ways I think I'm stuck in old paradigms and bound by old rules. I've lost three key employees in the past year. Each one wanted something I couldn't (or thought I couldn't) give—like a chance to telecommute two days a week or dress casually. Recently I saw another manager work out a deal with one of her prized employees. She got permission for him to work very different hours from everyone else. He's thrilled and producing like crazy. Now I'm rethinking my tendency to say no immediately to requests coming my way. Maybe I need to be more flexible in order to keep the talent on my team.

—Manager, hotel chain

ask yourself why. Is it a lack of trust in your employees? Is it concern that they will "goof off" or not be productive without your ever-vigilant eye? If so, consider managing based on results. Be clear about your expectations: what do you want them to produce or create? By when? Consider letting your employees get those results from whatever location they wish.

Space to Take a Break

A talented young engineer in a large aerospace firm asked his immediate boss for six weeks off work (without pay), to begin building his house. His boss said okay, even though the engineer's absence would certainly be a hardship. After the six weeks, the engineer asked for an additional four weeks, as he just hadn't done as much as he had hoped on his house. The boss pondered the request, thought about how valued this employee was, ran the request up to the division engineer, and came back with the okay. The engineer remained a loyal, committed employee for another 24 years. He later became a member of the senior management team and helped lead his company to tremendous success. When asked what he would have done had they turned down his request, he said he would have quit the job and found a new one after completing his project.

Seldom do we find managers who value their employees enough to allow them the space to take a real break from work. Yet in some countries and in certain fields (such as college teaching), sabbaticals are actually encouraged. Employers support valuable employees in their decisions to travel, learn something new, or simply go to the mountains and meditate. The next time your talented employee asks you for a break, get creative (with the employee) about finding a way to make it happen. Your employee will feel supported, and the odds of your retaining that talent will go up.

Space to Dress How One Wishes

We have all read about the high-tech environment in which people with creative, brilliant minds dress in all kinds of bizarre outfits. Some wonder if it is appropriate or professional or conducive to productivity. The results seem to speak for themselves. Just take a look at successful companies like Microsoft, where there are *no dress codes* in many departments. How productive have they been over the years? Managers in those environments say that their employees often work long hours (sometimes 70-hour weeks) by their own choosing, as they strive to complete a project or get a new product out the door. Allowing them to dress as they wish seems a small concession, considering the commitment and high productivity.

> *I don't feel I need to dress up to meet an equation.*
>
> —Aerospace engineer

Think about where you can offer flexibility in dress. Is it Friday-casual day? Summer attire? Different dress codes for those who never see a customer? Challenge the rules a bit. Are they reasonable? If business wear is truly necessary, then you will want to support the rule—but think about the requirements realistically and with a creative eye. It is truly amazing how favorably many employees view a flexible dress code.

Space to Design One's Space

Should all work areas in your organization look alike? Anyone who has studied personality differences knows that one way we express our uniqueness is in our surroundings. Our homes, our offices, and our cubicles will reflect our style if we are given the freedom.

Many organizations today hire interior decorating firms that design beautiful, perfect work areas. In some of those workplaces, the decorating rules are quite explicit, and there is no room for personalization. What about your organization? If the rules allow for some flexibility, then you as a manager have *room to allow space* for your employees. Let them bring in their favorite pictures and organize their desks the way they wish. Do not demand that everyone have work spaces like yours.

> One worker at Apple, a very visual thinker, was stumped when he was forced to sit at his computer to put down his thoughts. To help facilitate his thinking, his manager covered all the walls of his office with dry-erase board.
>
> *****
>
> Workers' cubicles could be their castles—with a little help. One manager gave his employees a small decorating stipend for personalizing their workplaces. They were thrilled, and have done some very creative things to make their cubes their castles.

Giving Inner Space

Space to Be Self-Directed and to Work and Think in New Ways

Giving inner space requires that managers *let go and trust* their talented employees to manage and continuously improve their work.

> The retail giant Nordstrom knows a lot about giving its employees space and empowering them to make decisions and manage their own work. In fact, managers credit their corporate culture for one of the highest retention rates in the retail industry. The primary rule, stated in Nordstrom's employee handbook, is this: Use your good judgment at all times.
>
> Because workers are empowered to make sure the customer is satisfied, Nordstrom customers typically experience remarkable service. The employee who ironed the new shirt a customer needed for a meeting and the one who gift-wrapped items a customer had

bought at Macy's are both examples of how Nordstrom employees provide great customer service. They have the space to manage their work in their own unique and creative ways.

A five-year employee with a record of superior customer service summed it up this way: "Where else could I get paid so well and have so much autonomy? Nordstrom is one of the first places I've ever felt like I really belong to something special. Sure I work really hard, but I like to work hard. No one tells me what to do, and I feel I can go as far as my dedication will take me. I feel like an entrepreneur." [55]

A pilot from Southwest Airlines and an accountant at Microsoft both relate similar stories of flexible environments with a minimum of bureaucracy. Both employees feel fortunate to have such a high level of control over their work. Although the pilot has very strict schedules to meet and clearly defined safety rules, he feels that his boss and the Southwest culture give him tremendous personal flexibility. The Microsoft accountant describes an environment that is typical in high-tech companies, where talent is hard to find and harder to keep. Employees' hours, physical space, dress, and *even the way they approach their tasks* are left up to each individual or team.

TO DO . . .

✓ Let your employees manage more aspects of their own work, without direct supervision.

✓ Trust them to get it right and then assist when they need your help.

✓ Allow them to try new ways of accomplishing their tasks, even if "it's never been done that way before."

You probably have more space as a manager to *give space to your employees* in this arena than in any other, and the payoff is tremendous. If you cannot offer telecommuting or casual dress codes, you *can* offer the power to manage the way they do the day-to-day work.

Space to Manage One's Own Time

All the research points to the fact that emerging workers (of any age) want flexibility in work schedules. A study by *Information Week* found flexibility to be second in importance to challenging work for IT (information technology) workers and managers.[56]

So what are organizations doing in response to these wants? According to Hewitt Associates, a human resources consulting firm, in 1990 about half of all employers studied offered some type of flexible scheduling. A decade later it was 74 percent.[57]

> *"Tasked with building a top-notch, diverse workforce, the Office of Personnel Management offers alternative work schedules as a way for federal agencies to increase productivity, lure talent away from the private sector and keep workers happy.*
>
> *"With the program, agencies can scrap traditional eight-hour days and 40-hour weeks in favor of arrangements tailored to individual needs. By striking a better balance on the personal/professional seesaw, workers are expected to achieve greater success on the job.*
>
> *"With nearly all agencies using flextime in some form, and with 1.8 million employees taking advantage of it, according to OPM's most recent count, managers have formed strong opinions about the program. Some love it. Others hate it. But most agree that it is a powerful human resources tool."*[58]

What if yours isn't one of these flex-friendly employers? This may be another area where you say, "I have no control. Our organization has strict policies about work hours and how and where they are spent." If that is true, then you will want to consider other ways of offering space to your employees. However, we encourage you to see where there *might* be some flexibility to offer your employees space to manage their work time according to their own unique needs. For example, one supervisor we know allowed workers to arrive ten minutes before their shifts began and leave ten minutes earlier or vice versa. He realized that this ten-minute window could substantially reduce driving time during rush hours, making a huge difference in his employees' stress.

What about Fairness?

Our readers have asked us about fairness. "How do I give one employee time off on Friday afternoon and not give it to everyone?" Being fair does not mean treating everyone identically.

Do you have more than one child? If so, do you give them all identical holiday gifts? Probably not.

The answer is mass customization (sounds like an oxymoron, doesn't it?), and it offers a new kind of institutional fairness. The workforce is more differentiated, and one policy simply does not fit all. (Who said management was easy?) Listen to your talented employees' requests, and brainstorm with them to create innovative solutions that are *fair*, both to them and to their hard-working, talented teammates—the ones you also want to keep!

Of course, there's a catch. Sure, you can take Friday off to train for the Ironman Triathlon or to attend your kid's soccer match. Just make sure you do your job—and figure out how to do it better than anyone else. With freedom and flexibility come responsibility and accountability—lots of it.

—Paula Lawlor, from MediHealth Outsourcing[59]

BOTTOM LINE

Job sharing, flextime, telecommuting, and designing one's own work space are not accommodation or pampering. They are ways to meet your business goals. That means listening to what people want, going to bat for their needs, and ultimately giving them options and opportunities to do things differently. Truly listen to the unique requests your employees bring you. Make an honest attempt to win flexibility and improved work conditions for your people.

Space to play, have a good time, take breaks, celebrate successes, creatively attack problems—all of this makes for a retention culture. Your reward will be loyalty and commitment from your best people.

Chapter 20

RUTH

Tell It

I can handle the truth. Why couldn't they just tell me?

—A.J.

Are you an honest person? Do you believe in telling the truth? Most people will answer "yes" to both questions. But think of how often you've told someone, "You look terrific!" when you didn't mean it. We know that honesty is the best policy, but that doesn't mean we always tell the truth.

Our studies show that employees yearn for straight talk. They want to *hear* the truth about their performance and the organization. They want to *tell you* the truth about your performance. When the truth is missing, people may feel demoralized, less confident in their leaders, and ultimately less loyal to the organization. Of course you know where that might lead—right out your door and through the competition's. Tell the truth if you want to engage and keep your good people.

A New View of Truth-Telling

The secret of truth-telling is to view it as a *gift*. If you believe that giving truthful, balanced feedback to people will help them to be more effective in their careers and perhaps in life, then you will be more in-clined to give that feedback.

Have you ever taken music or dance lessons or had a tennis or golf coach? Think back to that time and recall one of your lessons.

Did he demonstrate a better way to grip the racket or club? Did she help you develop better rhythm? Weren't they constantly helping you to fine-tune your approach? The feedback was probably balanced between *praise*—"That was great. Play it again just like that!"—and *correction*—"This time hold the bat more like this." Their gift was honest feedback, from someone willing to tell you there was still room for improvement and committed to helping you get there. Your employees expect and need the same kind of coaching from you today.

In fact, an interesting study done by Ohio State University's Fisher College of Business suggests that, in the absence of feedback, pay becomes more important. "When employees aren't given a lot of feed-back about how they are doing, they have to use pay as their only measure of worth. This magnifies the importance of salary as a way to feel appreciated and for employees to gauge their importance."[60]

Tell Them the Truth about Their Work

Think about the people who work with you or report to you. Consider their relative strengths and weaknesses, their blind spots, their overused strengths, and the flaws that may stall them. Have you been honest and direct about your perceptions with these people?

When and how did you give them your input? Even the best bosses might honestly confess that they have trouble giving people direct feed-back, especially about possible flaws or areas where employees need improvement. These managers may be concerned about hurting their employees' feelings, demoralizing them, or even prompting someone to quit because of negative feedback.

Most of us were not trained to give negative news. Our elders taught us that "honesty is the best policy," but we also learned, "If you can't say something nice, don't say anything at all." So we don't.

Alas

I honestly thought I was doing a great job. I had been promoted several times, had had positive performance reviews, and had received a bonus every year. The next thing I knew, I was passed over for a big promotion, shoved in a corner, and ignored. When the downsizing happened, I was laid off. Only then did I hear that there had been some problems with my management style through the years.

—Unemployed middle manager

The Truth Hurts, or Does It?

When employees in most organizations are asked what they would like more of from their managers, their first response is usually *feedback.* People want to know where they stand—they want to know if your perception of their performance is the same as their own.

Years of research (much of it done by the Center for Creative Leadership) confirms that the absence of honest feedback derails leaders at all levels. Sometimes that means getting fired, but more often it means failing to achieve what a person was believed capable of achieving.[61] Even the high potentials in your organization need honest, balanced feedback. Too often they hear only how wonderful, bright, and talented they are. Without feedback, these employees can come to a startling, shocking halt after several promotions, big raises, and starring roles. Why? Because no one helped them see their rough edges and the need for continual improvement. They began to believe their own press and developed major blind spots. Their confidence turned into arrogance, in part because of insufficient, inaccurate, imbalanced, or tardy feedback from key people in their lives. The truth could have saved them.

TO DO . . .

✓ Within the next 30 days, give honest feedback to each of your employees, including the high-potentials and solid citizens.

In many organizations, managers are only required to give feedback during the annual performance review. They give input to reward and reinforce employees' behaviors and performance, to justify the annual raise, or to warn them about unsatisfactory performance and possible consequences. Some managers gloss over the negatives and focus on the good news only, and others do just the opposite. In either case, the reviews don't tell the whole truth, and employees are often left frustrated by the whole process.

Consider these two points:

✓ Formal performance appraisal meetings are important. If they are handled badly, your employees may feel dismissed and unimportant. Plan carefully and balance the good news (positive) with the important news (room for improvement).

✓ Don't give feedback just once a year. To retain your key people, it is essential that you give regular, honest feedback.

Alas

In our organization, the employee and boss both fill out the performance appraisal form once a year. The idea is to compare results and have a discussion about the employee's performance and where he might improve. I spent hours filling mine out, really trying to evaluate my strengths and weaknesses and how I had done in reaching my goals. I turned it in to my boss three weeks before our "big meeting." When I showed up, it became clear that he had not looked at my report at all and had filled in his form in a hurry, just minutes before the meeting. All the ratings were just average, and when I asked him how I could bring them up, he said he would have to think about it. Twenty minutes later he said he had another meeting. So—I had waited all year to get feedback from my boss, and when it finally came, it was mediocre and almost meaningless. I have never felt so insignificant—maybe I need to start looking around for another job.

—Nursing supervisor, hospital

"What If I Don't Know How?"

Many managers are uncomfortable giving feedback (positive or negative) because they don't know how to do it simply and effectively. Many have never had a good role model. Giving feedback so that it doesn't put employees on the defensive is key. How do you measure up? Take this quiz to see if you are feedback-savvy.

Feedback Quiz

My feedback . . .

✓ Is private. (I choose a place where the person can hear my comments without being distracted or embarrassed.)

_____ True _____ False

✓ Receives the time it deserves. (I plan the time and use it just for the purpose of giving feedback to someone.)

_____ True_____ False

✓ Is frequent. (I give feedback immediately after actions that need to be changed or rewarded.)

_____ True_____ False

✓ Focuses more on the future than the past. (I talk mostly about what can be done to improve, rather than what went wrong.)

_____ True_____ False

✓ Is specific, with clear examples. ("I think you need to delegate more. You did all of last quarter's project yourself.")

_____ True_____ False

✓ Gives information that helps the person to make decisions. ("Your team wants you to involve them more in planning.")

_____ True_____ False

✓ Gives suggestions for growth and improvement. ("I think you could work on negotiating skills, especially if you want that new role.")

_____ True_____ False

✓ Allows for discussion. ("Tell me what you are thinking. What do you want to do about this?")

_____ True_____ False

✓ Creates next steps. ("Let's meet again next week to create a development plan for you. Meanwhile, think about what you'd like to include in that plan.")

_____ True_____ False

How did you do? If most of these statements are true for you, fantastic! Now go ask your employees if they agree. Ask them to tell you the truth.

Confidentially Speaking

Another approach that is gaining in popularity is 360-degree feedback: employees receive feedback from you, their peers, mentors, customers, and direct reports. That feedback is about their competencies (skills, behaviors, attitudes, and traits) and is very specific. It highlights both strengths and opportunities to improve, and its purpose is developmental. Because it is usually anonymous, raters tend to be very honest. It is valuable for all of us to get input from someone other than the boss; 360-degree feedback is just one way of doing that. For a comprehensive look at leadership development and 360-degree feedback, see *The Leadership Machine* by Michael Lombardo and Robert Eichinger.[62]

Note: Be sure to follow up with coaching and support for people who get critical feedback about behaviors they need to change. Getting the feedback is usually just the first step; most people will need help creating and implementing a development plan.

TO DO . . .

✓ If you have an employee who is having difficulty believing that he has weaknesses, consider using 360-degree feedback. Your human resources professional should be able to help you choose the most appropriate tool.

see INFORMATION

Tell Them the Truth about the Organization

Research overwhelmingly supports the notion that engaged employees are "in the know." They want to be trusted with the truth about the business, including its challenges and downturns.

We know, however, that there may be times when you are simply not at liberty to tell the whole truth. A pending merger, reorganization, or change at the top of the organization could be off-limits for discussion with your team.

Managers sometimes hold information back in the belief that it makes them more powerful or that it is better for their employees not to know. When you have bad news, give it face-to-face and as soon as possible. If you make a mistake, confess, tell them the truth, and accept responsibility. Your personal stock will go up and so will the trust level on your team.

Ask Them for the Truth (Even about You)

We would rather be ruined by praise then saved by criticism.
—Norman Vincent Peale

So far we've been talking about telling the truth to your employees. But what about getting them to tell you the truth? Many managers (especially at high levels) have had no formal performance reviews or feedback sessions for years. By the time they rise to the top, they might be getting almost no balanced, accurate input about *how* they get the work done. Often, leaders are rewarded as long as they hit their bottom-line targets.

Who then tells the senior leader about his warts? (Or the emperor about his clothes?) Probably no one. That absence of truthful, balanced feedback creates leaders who have missed the opportunity to grow, to be even more effective in their jobs, and to keep their talented people.

In almost every setting outside the modern American organization, the experts and masters continue to ask for the truth about their performance, and they strive for improvement. Athletes, musicians, and martial arts masters are examples of this practice. *You* can establish an environment where truth is welcome. And you can serve as a model for your employees as they watch how you *seek and receive* feedback. View it as a gift.

BOTTOM LINE

Telling the truth is a healthy philosophy, both personally and professionally. People who hear the truth about themselves and the organization and feel free to tell *you* the truth, are more engaged and more likely to stay.

Chapter 21

# UNDERSTAND

Listen Deeper

My boss never really understood me.

—A.J.

"You're not listening. You *never* listen." If you ever hear these complaints, at home or at work, read on. Why is there no end to the training courses on this subject? Why do feedback surveys repeatedly tell managers that they are lousy listeners? Why don't we *get it?*

Most managers don't really believe that listening is a critical skill. They believe that being results-oriented or customer-focused is much more important to business success than being a good listener. Are they right?

> Joe understands me. He listens to me—and I feel understood. The more he listens, the more I reveal, and the stronger our relationship becomes. We have developed a huge amount of trust. With other bosses, I used to edit. I tell Joe everything. As a result, he is never surprised. He has a better handle on things. Because of our bond, we are more creative, take bigger risks, push the boundaries, and accomplish amazing things. I have never had a better boss, and I have never been so productive. Right now, nothing could entice me away from this job.
>
> —Senior vice president, engineering organization

Research confirms our belief that an unsatisfactory work relationship with the manager is one of the major reasons people leave.

TO DO ...

✓ Stop now and write down three or four things you learned from your employees this week. It could be a process improvement idea, a customer challenge, or a team issue. If you can't list three or four, you probably have not been listening carefully enough to your employees.

Communication is critical to keeping your talent. If they feel heard, understood, and valued by you, they will work harder and produce more. They will *want* to stay and work for you. And if they don't—they will disengage or depart.

> *"He'll sit there and listen. I mean, really listen. He's in our corner. That takes the load off. Then when you go on the football field and the man says, 'Look, I want you to run down there, catch that ball and run into that wall, then who are you to say no'? You catch that ball and you run into that wall. You say, 'Okay, Coach, you were there for me; now I'm gonna give it up for you.' That's crucial."*
> —Michael Irvin, Dallas Cowboys[63]

Tune Out—Miss Out

The manager's head moves up and down. She says, "Uh-huh," 35 times in a row. Is she listening? Probably not. So what gets in the way of listening deeper? What are you thinking about while your employee talks?

TO DO ...

Which of these do you sometimes think while your employees talk to you? Be honest.

✓ I already know the punch line. I'm five steps ahead.
✓ I'm too busy for this. I have a stack of work on my desk.
✓ He's getting emotional. I'm checking out.
✓ I wonder how my son is doing in school today.
✓ Now what should my response be? How can I defend my position?
✓ She's so boring. I'm going to plan my meeting while she talks.

How did you do? You might believe that it is great time management (multitasking) to have your mind busy while another person talks or to be planning your response so that you are ready the minute the employee stops speaking. You might be impatient. You might believe that your time and ideas are worth more than your employee's. Or you may have just forgotten how to really focus on a person and listen deeply. Regardless of your reason, the result is the same. *When you tune out, you miss out.* You miss out on information. More importantly, you miss out on having a respectful relationship.

Listening Is a Choice

You might already have great listening skills and habits, but you are selective about when you use them. Be conscious about how you are listening to your employees. Decide to listen deeper. Truly try to understand your talented people.

> *What stands out most, and what kept me at that company for many years, was really a simple thing. Every Friday we'd get together at a local pub, and the general manager would come in and start the party with one question, "So, how was your week?" We'd all go on and on about the problems we had faced, the successes we'd had, the issues that we still had to deal with. We didn't really solve much (although that happened occasionally). Mostly we all just vented. And the amazing thing was, he was truly interested. We went home those weekends feeling great.*
>
> —Employee, furniture retail company

Listen Up

Experts have been writing about the importance of listening in the world of work . . . forever! Still, it remains one of the biggest complaints on the part of employees everywhere. Kenny Moore, in his book *The CEO and the Monk*, suggests that listening has become a lost art in business. "Become a better communicator by keeping your mouth shut. We risk creating a culture where the ones that speak the most and the loudest win out. My instincts tell me that that's not going to satisfy our customers, whether external or internal. There is something to be said for maintaining a quiet demeanor. Silence on our part invites the thoughts and opinions of others, a true recipe for sustained growth and competitive advantage."[64]

Most of us spend little time listening to truly understand and aren't sure how to develop that skill. Here is one way.

The Blinking Word

Many managers are becoming better listeners by learning a simple technique called the *blinking word*. Here is how it works.

> *Scenario:* Your employee, Shelby, asks to talk to you, so you schedule a meeting in your office. You welcome Shelby in and ask what you can do for her. She says, "I'm having trouble with one of my employees. He seems to lack motivation for the job."

1. Identify the words that blink (stand out).
   *"I'm having **trouble** with one of my employees. He seems to **lack motivation** for the job."*

2. Ask about one of the blinking words.
   "What kind of trouble?" or *"How does he seem to lack motivation?"*

3. Listen for Shelby's answer.
   *"He's not as **productive** as he used to be."*

4. Notice the blinking word in her answer and question it.
   "How has his productivity dropped?"

5. Listen for Shelby's answer.
   *"He gets **less** work done in a week, and the **quality** has **slipped** too."*

6. Notice the blinking word in her answer and question it.
   "Why do you think he is getting less work done?" or "Tell me about the slip in quality."

7. Keep going, watch for the blinking words, and ask about them.

Use open questions as you follow the blinking words. Open questions begin with words like *how, why, where, when, tell me about.* By following the blinking word, you go deeper into Shelby's problem. Meanwhile, Shelby feels listened to. She believes that you care about her dilemma and are there to help her solve it. The blinking word technique will force you to listen empathetically, at the deepest level. You will not be able to tune in and out and still follow the blinking word. (P.S. *Do* try this at home. Your spouse, kids, and friends will be pleasantly surprised at what a good listener you have become.)

Alas

I watched him read his mail while his employees talked to him. I was on the receiving end of that behavior a few times myself. He probably thought we didn't notice or that we respected his ability to multitask. He was wrong. We felt unimportant and unheard most of the time.

—Frontline employee

Listening Liabilities

These deterrents to effective listening may prevent you from understanding your employees and, ultimately, from keeping them on your team.

The Interrupter

Have you ever tried to have a conversation with someone who finishes your sentences or interrupts with their own brilliant thought about the topic? Your employees will lose patience with you and may quit coming to you with their ideas and challenges if you interrupt them at every turn.

Notice when you interrupt your employees. Use the blinking word technique. Let them do the talking while you do the listening. Give them credit for great ideas and *let them finish.*

The Defender

Defensive listeners also interrupt. They may be defending their thinking, their stand on a topic, the status quo, or their status or role in the organization. Notice if you are a defender. Stop and let your employees explain their thinking or their position on a topic. Try to really understand them before you rush to your own defense.

The Transmitter

Some people seem to transmit only. They spend more time talking than listening. What percentage of the time are you typically talking? Twenty percent? Eighty percent? Someone once said that we were given two ears and one mouth for a reason—we should be listening twice as much as we are talking. Try giving your employees a chance to say more.

Listen Deeper

> *"Every person I work with knows something better than I—my job is to listen long enough to find it and use it."*
>
> —Jack Nicolaus

Some managers wonder, "What should I be listening for?" We believe it is important to listen for

✓ **Input.** Talented people want to have an ear for their great ideas and solutions. They want to be heard and recognized.

see REWARD

> *My boss not only listened to my ideas, but she let me present them at the board meeting. I felt so proud.*
>
> —Manager, real estate management firm

✓ *Motivations.* What do they want from this job and from you? What gets them up in the morning and looking forward to their work?

He asked me what I liked about the job and what I wasn't so thrilled with. He listened. Once he really understood where I was coming from, he suggested that we hand off some of my least favorite tasks to a colleague who likes doing that work. He seems to really understand me.

—Supervisor, medical group

✓ *Challenges.* You need to know about your employees' problems and challenges.

One of my direct reports has a talented employee named Denise. Her performance level had dropped, and we were wondering why. I suggested that we both meet with her. We asked Denise if something was bothering her, and she began to talk. Finally she shared that she was battling cancer but had been afraid to tell us. We listened to her for two hours. She said that she felt so much better now that the secret was out, and she thanked us for our support and understanding. That was two years ago. Denise has made it through the tough times and has recently been promoted.

—Director, advertising firm

Some of our readers have said they are uncomfortable listening deeply, especially about employees' lives outside of work. They fear heartfelt conversations may take them to a personal level or an empathetic state that leaves them vulnerable.

Some managers don't want their people to discuss their personal lives at all. I say, bring it on. If people can get something off their chest for an hour, I've got them for the next 20 (or more)."

—Team leader, small manufacturing plant

*****

I hire knowledge workers. I need their brainpower. If they are unhappy with me, the organization, or their personal lives, they show up at

work with half a brain. I can't afford that. I listen to their problems,
help them brainstorm solutions, and refer them to helpful resources.
I work very hard to keep them happy.

—Executive, high-tech company

You don't have to play counselor, and you don't have to have answers to their personal problems. Just listen.

Getting to Know Them

It's not too late to learn how to listen more effectively and learn more about the talented people you want to keep. Think of yourself as an archaeologist on a dig. Take your curiosity to the relationship and see what you can learn.

TO DO . . .

✓ Invite employees you do not know well to have lunch with you. Ask about them and their interests. Practice listening.

✓ Accept style differences among your employees. Listen to your slow talkers as well as the fast ones.

✓ Listen and act on ideas your employees bring you. When they see that you have implemented one of their ideas, they will feel heard.

✓ Notice little things. Go to your employees' work spaces and take note of the family pictures or sports trophies. Ask about them.

✓ Open your door. One employee said, "Sometimes I'd walk into my boss's office stressed and uptight. He would say, 'What do you need, some listening time?' I always felt like he accepted me and understood me."

✓ Slow down and listen. Sometimes managers are just moving too quickly (mentally and physically) to get to know and understand their employees.

✓ Clear your desk so you can focus on your employee, not the latest report you need to read.

✓ Notice your employee's eye color. This will help you connect eye-to-eye with that person.

✓ Remember to use the blinking word technique to listen deeper.

✓ If they bring you personal problems that are outside of your expertise or your boundaries as their manager, brainstorm with them to come up with a list of potential resources (such as counselors, human resource professionals, and community service organizations).

BOTTOM LINE

Strive to understand your employees by really listening to them. Pay attention to your own listening style and improve it (there's always room). Your efforts will pay off. Employees who feel heard and understood will stay engaged and on your team. Those who don't will find another place to work, with a boss who *will* listen.

Chapter 22

VALUES

Define and Align

I don't think my manager really understood what I value most. I felt like I had to leave my real self at home.

—A.J.

The risk of losing employees because of conflicts over values is far greater than the risk of losing them because of compensation. Values define what we consider to be important. They are the standards by which we measure our bottom-line needs. The more your employees' work incorporates their values, the more they will find that work meaningful, purposeful, and important. And, of course, it follows that the more this is the case, the longer they will stay.

How do your employees' values align with the organizational values? Do you know? Organizations have vision statements, mission statements, and values statements, but they rarely have a process that helps employees determine the link between those statements and their own values.

Values are the emotional salary of work, and some folks are drawing no wages at all.

—Howard Figler

The Importance of Aligning Values

Did you know that you and your employees spend more time working than doing almost anything else, including sleeping? They want to spend that time doing something they truly value.

When values are left out of the work equation, the work may still get done, but without the energy and commitment. Eventually, either you or your employees will notice. Today's employees across all generations want to find value and meaning in their work. Our lives aren't as compartmentalized as they once were, and more employees are demanding a better blending of work and home life. Learning about the values that matter to your employees may be a tall order for a manager, but not an impossible one.

TO DO...

For clues to employees' values, try any of the following to start a conversation:

✓ What do you need most from your work? Does the job deliver?
✓ What makes for a really good day?
✓ What would you miss if you left this job?
✓ What did you like best about other jobs you've had?
✓ What small steps can we take to incorporate more of your values?
✓ How do you most like to spend your time outside of work?
✓ Tell me about a time when you really felt energized at work.

"We're Not in Kansas Anymore"

Nearly every employee who's been restructured, reengineered, or reorganized can relate to Dorothy in *The Wizard of Oz*. Events way beyond their control, much like the cyclone, have whirled them around and deposited them in a strange land. The employee thinks, "I'm not in control. I didn't ask to be in this place. I hope I like it."

In any change, human nature and the need to pay the rent generally force us to adapt as quickly as possible. The problem comes about 120 days later as some employees begin to realize that adapting is costing them dearly. And that sense of loss is almost always a values-related problem.

"Employees have always looked for personal satisfaction, but what may have changed in this decade is what personal satisfaction means," according to a program manager for a manufacturing firm in California. "People have really taken us back to the drawing board to revisit the top priorities in our lives. The challenge for a corporate culture, when people are visiting their values closely, is to offer flexibility within the company's demands."[65]

VALUES
Define and Align

203

Alas

We were once conducting a career development workshop at the corporate headquarters of a large, multinational bank. The participants were considered to be the future leadership of the bank—all labeled as high-potential—and the bank was investing heavily in their future. We were using an instrument called "Invest in Your Values."[66] Each participant was to choose seven values important to him or her from a field of 35 and apply colored stickers to them. The stickers indicated whether the value was being delivered (green sticker), was not being delivered but could be negotiated for or made to happen (yellow sticker), or was not possible in the future—no matter what. Those got a red sticker.

As we walked around the room observing the choices people made and noticing the colored stickers, we were happy to see mostly green stickers. This indicated high satisfaction in the values delivery department. A few yellows—okay, they can be fixed and, for these high-potentials, heaven itself would be moved to fix them.

(continued)

> *But there was one red sticker on the board in front of an angry-looking young man. He pounded the red sticker down as though he was punishing the offending value itself. This young man had been pointed out to us as a shining star and an important "acquisition." He was hired particularly for his innovative thinking. And he was the only person in a room of more than 30 people who had a red sticker on one of his highest-rated values. The offending sticker was slapped onto the value word* creativity. *He had indicated this to be an extremely important value. When we asked him why he put the red sticker on creativity, he said (with great vehemence), "Because you can't be creative in this bank!"*

The very reason he had been hired was the reason they would lose him. If his manager had been willing to have a conversation about values with this high-potential employee, he might have been able to figure out just what the creativity-stifling problem was.

If the manager were particularly brave, another response to the creativity comment could be, "What role have I played? What could I do differently to support you?" It takes guts, but those questions, if handled well, could prevent a high-potential employee from leaving.

How can you determine which values can help you retain your employees? You can give them a self-paced values-analysis instrument like the one used in the *Alas* story or invent your own. You can make it part of your next staff meeting or ask them any of these questions to stimulate a conversation:

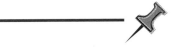

TO DO . . .

see UNDERSTAND

Show employees this list of value choices. Listen to their responses and dig deeper where you can.

✓ When you go to work, you look forward to
   a. Having new challenges.
   b. Enjoying the company of coworkers.
   c. Planning your own day.
   d. A relaxed, routine day.

✓ When you have a new project to work on, you're excited if
   a. You will learn new things.
   b. You will get to work with new people.
   c. You will be in control.
   d. It will be easy and low stress.

✓ If you won the lottery, one thing that might keep you from quitting your job would be
   a. The excitement of competition.
   b. Missing friends at work.
   c. Having work goals to motivate you.
   d. Not knowing what to do with your time.

✓ In your ideal job, you would
   a. Have opportunities to be creative.
   b. Help society.
   c. Start your own business.
   d. Never work more than eight hours a day.

✓ Looking back, you felt most satisfied with work when
   a. You were involved in exciting projects.
   b. You were helping others.
   c. You worked totally independently.
   d. You never had to take work home.

✓ You work best when
   a. Your curiosity and energy are high.
   b. You're working with a team.
   c. You're working primarily alone.
   d. There are no deadlines.

✓ Success, to you, means
   a. Always pursuing excellence.
   b. Working closely with friends.
   c. Being the master of your own future.
   d. Being content with your work.

A Quick Guide That Might Guide You:

"A" answers suggest that these people are goal-oriented. Help them find opportunities to work on stimulating projects that lead to clear-cut results and a sense of accomplishment.

"B" answers suggest that these employees are people oriented. Look for ways to increase their interpersonal contacts at work, perhaps through participation on task forces and project teams.

"C" answers indicate self-starters. Find situations that reward self-motivation with even more freedom and independence. Don't micromanage these people.

"D" answers suggest that these people seek balance and an orderly work routine. Good soldiers, these people will need the greatest attention and reassurance during change.

Value the Differences on Your Team

Organizations are more team-based than ever. Yet the failure to understand one another's values leads to discord on teams. The team that cannot draw on its members' values may end up arguing, wasting time, and failing. Team members lose heart when organizational values and *their* values do not mesh. Be aware of the individual values on your team and be willing to discuss them. You will strengthen the group and increase its members' job satisfaction.

Since the team itself is a major retention factor, an individual's values are worth your consideration and action. First be sure you recognize your own values—and their impact on your employees. We have looked at hundreds of transcripts from exit interviews. We were amazed at how many talented employees left because their values conflicted with those of their immediate supervisor or manager. Are you aware of the values conflicts you may have with those on your team?

Sometimes as managers we tend to project our values onto our employees. But diversity of values will build strength in your team. Those who value creativity will be your innovators. Those who value independence will work productively for long stretches without prodding from you. Those who value order and routine will be your dependable, solid citizens. Don't try to make the solid citizen into a creative innovator. Recognize what each person values and mine those values for the sake of the whole team.

TO DO . . .

Consider talking about values with your team. One or more of these questions might get the conversation rolling:

✓ What are the values of our work team? How are we similar? How are we different?
✓ How might our differences get in the way?
✓ Under what circumstances or pressures do we find our values colliding?
✓ What can we learn from someone whose values are different from our own?
✓ It's easy to feel judgmental about value differences. How does that impact the group?

Finding *Their* Calling

If the area of values interests you, there are many books about how to help individuals find their calling, their passion, or their personal or professional mission. In their book *Whistle While You Work: Heeding Your Life's Calling*, Dick Leider and David Shapiro suggest that people who have a powerful calling about their work tend to love what they do and experience a level of joy on the job that most of us only dream of.[67] You could have your entire team read the book, and then discuss what they found meaningful in it. This could provoke a discussion about values.

BOTTOM LINE

The match between your employees' values and the organization's or team's values is a more powerful factor by far than money in keeping good people. How satisfied are your talented people with their everyday tasks? Do you know enough about your employees' values to answer that question? Values are not difficult to uncover, but they are powerful forces in an employee's decision to stay or leave. Imagine your employees as your customers. Now, what do they value most? How can you help them attain it?

Chapter 23

WELLNESS

Sustain It

To be successful there meant giving up my health and my fun, and I was not willing to do that.

—A.J.

Does your organization insist on yearly physicals? Does it invest in gymnasiums, volleyball courts, or stress management workshops? If you're laughing, keep reading. Companies that take wellness seriously find that the payoff is great, not only in retention, but also in energy for the job and in productivity. But this chapter is not about what the corporation can do. We are interested in how you, the manager, can enhance your team's wellness.

We're not kidding ourselves. We know that by virtue of simply doing business in today's fiercely competitive environment, like it or not, we contribute to the stress that complicates our lives. But rather than searching for a place to lay the blame, we choose to be part of the solution that makes it possible for these two very demanding worlds to coexist.

—Richard P. Kearns, from PricewaterhouseCoopers LLP

Wellness and Survival of the Fit

Today's workplace is typically high-energy and highly productive. To play successfully within it, you and your employees must be *well and fit,* mentally, emotionally, and physically. In this competitive environment, wellness is a "must have" rather than a "nice to have." Without it you simply will not win. By focusing on your employees' wellness, you can increase the odds that they will stay and play effectively on your team.

What Is Wellness?

To one person, wellness means that he can enter the Boston marathon and finish in four hours. To another, it may mean finally being free of migraine headaches. To another, it may mean slimming down or reducing stress and high blood pressure before the next physical exam.

   We define wellness as a *state of physical, mental, and emotional fitness.* To capture a clear picture of it, you might need to think back to a recent vacation when you felt incredibly relaxed, physically healthy and energetic, mentally sharp (maybe even creative), and emotionally satisfied. It may seem unreasonable to expect that you or your employees will feel at work like you feel on vacation, but it is useful to have the "perfect world" scenario in mind as you strive to increase your employees' fitness and wellness levels.

   Show interest in your employees' well-being. Here's what we are talking about.

see UNDERSTAND

Alas (almost)

Yolanda had recently missed several days of work and seemed uncharacteristically quiet and distant at her job. She was typically vivacious and fun-loving, and she often cheered up other team members with sagging spirits. Yolanda was still getting her work done, so her manager resisted

(continued)

saying anything to her about her absences or the shifts in her mood. Besides, he was concerned that to question her might somehow be crossing a line from the work world to the private world, and that seemed risky to him. So he said nothing.

Three months later Yolanda tearfully handed her manager her resignation. He was shocked and told her that he did not want her to go, that he and the entire team valued her highly. She seemed surprised by his response and said so. "I thought you didn't care about me at all, since you never asked why I was missing work or why I seemed so sad when I did show up. I assumed that the team would be better off without me."

Yolanda's boss finally did what she had wanted him to do weeks earlier. He did not pry but just offered to help. Yolanda began to cry (this time with gratitude) and explained that she was having health problems and that her responsibilities as a mother and a member of his team were just more than she could handle. She said that it was the stress of balancing everything that was getting her down, not the illness itself.

Within minutes, a talented employee's resignation turned into a plan for how Yolanda would manage her work and family responsibilities while she regained her health. The plan included working from home two days a week, as well as beginning work earlier in the morning and going home early in the afternoon to take a nap. Yolanda's loyalty and commitment to her boss and her team skyrocketed, her productivity remained high, and within a few months she was back on her original schedule and feeling great.

Yolanda's boss did the right thing in the nick of time for Yolanda, the team, and himself. He asked what he could do and then brainstormed solutions with his valuable employee. You can bet that Yolanda will not be easily enticed away to a new team or opportunity. The only thing he could have done better would have been to talk to her earlier.

Whether your employee faces a physical problem, stress, or an emotional challenge, your response as a manager can be the same. Ask how you can help and then collaborate on a plan.

TO DO . . .

✓ Notice if something is wrong or if your employees' work habits change dramatically. Do not wait. Ask if there is anything you can do to help. How simple it seems and how few managers do this.

One of my most talented engineers was having major temper flare-ups and causing a lot of turmoil on the team. My boss suggested I fire him. I decided that this employee was important enough to invest in. We talked, and I referred him to the Employee Assistance Program, where he got the help he needed. He has dealt with whatever was bothering him and is a joy to work with again. My supporting him through this proved to be an important statement to him and also to the team. We are stronger and more productive than ever.

—Engineering manager

✓ When an employee does tell you what is wrong, partner with that person to create a plan to remedy the situation.

The "B" Word

Most of us need a job, and all of us want a life. We should be able to have both.

A job satisfaction poll of 2,500 employees conducted by the Society for Human Resource Management (SHRM) and USAToday.com suggests that employees value work environments that support work/life balance, rating it fourth on an importance list. Compensation/pay came in fifth.[68] Another study by Tickle Inc. found that Americans would take 15 percent less pay for a better work/life balance.[69]

Balance between work and personal life contributes to wellness and constantly challenges the wellness-minded manager. One team we know has spent so much time in recent years dealing with the issue of balance that they now call it the "B" word. It is almost off-limits as a discussion topic because it seems there are few solutions, and they became "sick of talking about it."

We believe, though, that you *need to talk about it*—and think about it—and even do something about it! What does balance mean to you and to your employees? (It is different for everyone.)

One plant manager we heard about gives each of the 90 members of his team $150 a year to do something (anything!) to bring balance into their lives. His only request: tell me how you've used the money. The ways in which employees spend the money underscore how individual our balance needs are. Employees report spending their money on ballroom dance lessons, a drum set, gardening tools, and instruction in tai chi and kickboxing. One hundred fifty dollars per person is not a lot for him to spend, and the message he sends is crystal-clear. Do you have a discretionary budget that you might spend this way?

We are not suggesting that your employees' balance issues are your concern alone or that you must provide the answers. We are suggesting, however, that you can take actions to encourage balance and thus wellness.

Imagine life as a game in which you are juggling five balls in the air. You name them—work, family, health, friends, and spirit— you're keeping all of these in the air. You will soon understand that work is a rubber ball. If you drop it, it will bounce back. But the other four balls—family, health, friends, and spirit—are made of glass. If you drop one of these, it will be irrevocably scuffed, marked, nicked, damaged, or even shattered. It will never be the same. You must understand that.

—Brian Dyson, from Coca-Cola

Overwhelm Is an Understatement

"One of the early warning signs of stress is physical and mental fatigue. Some 49 percent of workers report that they are so stressed on the job that they often feel incapacitated, according to a 2004 survey of workers by ComPsych, a Chicago-based employee-assistance provider. More than a third say they lose an hour a day of productivity because they have difficulty concentrating; 44 percent admit to showing up for work up to four days a year too stressed to be effective."[70]

The pressures to do more with less, to move faster than the competition, to be more creative, more innovative, more distinct, to do it with fewer dollars, and to be available at all times push many to say that work just asks too much.

Alas

A senior manager in a healthcare organization noticed that he was snapping at his employees, having trouble sleeping, and feeling generally sluggish. When a friend asked him how he was spending his time away from work, he answered, "What time away from work?" In the past he had spent evenings at home and had enjoyed movies, friends, books, and music to relax. He had worked out at the gym four nights a week. All of that seemed a distant memory now. His new boss had set the tone: Those who are even remotely ambitious or committed to the organization work late every night. So much for balance and wellness. The results for this senior manager included his employees' being fed up with his grumpiness (two had recently quit), lower productivity than ever (maybe because he was exhausted), constant headaches, and increasing resentment toward his boss and the organization. Recently he has begun to check out the Internet job postings, thinking that there must be a saner place to work! This senior manager will be gone soon, having found a workplace where balance is at least a topic of discussion and where his boss expects that people have a life outside of work.

So what about you? What example do you set as a manager, and what do you expect from your people? Ask yourself these questions:

✓ Do I promote workaholism? Am I a workaholic?
✓ Do I expect my employees to travel or work on weekends? How often?
✓ Do I hold numerous early morning or early evening meetings?
✓ Do I compliment employees for their long hours or, instead, for the quality work they complete?

How did you do? Often managers discourage balance by the examples they set or by what they expect and reward.

TO DO . . .

✓ *Set the example you want them to follow.* If you want them to have more balance in their lives, you have to model it. Share what you do to achieve balance in your life. Your employees may think that you have none. (We hope they're wrong.)
✓ *Hold a balance discussion* at your next staff meeting (or in one-on-one meetings). Dedicate the whole meeting to the topic.
✓ *Ask people what they juggle* in their lives and what matters most to them. (Be ready to hear that work is *not the number one priority* for many of them.)
✓ *Support your employees in achieving balance.* Encourage the activities that they love; ask about their golf lessons or their children's school plays.

Stretched and Stressed

Hans Selye, the founder of the field of stress management, said, "To be free of stress is to be dead." We agree that just *living* is often stressful. But

Selye and others have found that, although optimum levels of stress produce peak performance, overdoses can definitely lead to poor performance and even to illness.

In organizations, we seldom see too little stress. We sometimes see the optimum stress level and high performance results. Most often, however, we see stress overload and negative results on health and on productivity. There seems to be a high correlation between lack of balance and stress. Where balance is missing, the workload typically appears to be very high and stressful. When people have balanced lives, they seem to have less work stress, or they just manage it better.

> *He seemed so uptight and distracted. I called him in to my office and asked if there was anything I could do. He confided in me. Well, actually, he just started venting! I listened and empathized as he poured out his frustration, anger, and disappointment. An hour later, he thanked me, said he felt 100 percent better and headed back to work. I guess he just needed for me to listen and quietly support him.*
>
> —Manager, manufacturing company

TO DO . . .

✓ Watch for signs of excess stress. When you think you see it in your employees, ask them how they are doing (or feeling). They will appreciate your asking and may confide in you.

✓ Once you know what's going on, brainstorm possible solutions *with* your employees. Be open and willing to think creatively as you search for ways to relieve stress. Consider some of these stress management options with them:

  • Shift some of the work to others if possible. Think about who could help and how to ask for the help.

  • Take more breaks. Get up, move around, go for a quick walk.

  • Take a break from "electronic leashes"—declare a Blackberry-free Wednesday morning.

- Learn relaxation, visualization, or breathing techniques. Take a stress management class or Yoga.
- Exercise as a way to relieve stress. Join a gym or take up power walking or jogging.
- Implement "no meetings on Fridays." Think of the work you could get done!
- Seek professional help or counseling.
- Get enough sleep, eat well, and reduce stress-producing chemicals like caffeine and nicotine.
- Take a vacation—a real one. One manager we know tells his people not to check voice mail or e-mail! (Yes, that means you'd need to have back-up support.)

✓ Support your employees as they practice stress management. For example, if Mike decides he needs to take two 15-minute brisk walks during the day to relieve stress, be sure that you reward his actually doing it. Your support will pay off.

✓ Take a good look at the role you play. Stop calling your employees at night—give them a break.

✓ Take a stand to reduce stress on your team. Coach the managers who report to you. Reward and hold them accountable for reducing, not increasing, the stress of their workers.

BOTTOM LINE

Savvy managers view work/life balance and stress reduction initiatives as strategic business tools, not as employee perks. If your employees are well and feel a balance between work and life outside of work, you are far more likely to have a well-functioning organization. Your best employees will work hard, produce for you, *and stick around* in an environment that promotes their health and fitness—emotional, mental, and physical.

Chapter 24

X-ers and Other Generations

Handle with Care

I saw three young talented employees pack their bags and leave, mostly because we were just too rigid and tended to micromanage them. We should have loosened up a bit.

—A.J.

WARNING! This chapter contains generalizations that reflect research into the attitudes and behaviors of the age groups now in the U.S. workforce. We are not recommending that you manage each of your employees according to these generalizations without taking employee individuality into account. But we do want to give you potentially useful information about patterns that fall within generational lines. Our intent is not to label people but to offer guidelines for your thinking so you can keep your best people.

Does your organization invest in researching the ages and demographic characteristics of your customers? Consumer research specialists and marketing experts use that knowledge to better serve that group or sell their product or service. In trying to keep your best people, aren't you really trying to serve and sell as well? And wouldn't it be useful to better understand the characteristics that help define a group of people or differentiate them? Knowledge of generations at work will help you do just that.

Here's an example of using generational knowledge to deliver what your employees want, across generations.

Assumption: Your talented workers, of any age, want flexibility. Here's how the generations might think about and define *flexibility* differently from one another. Notice the nuances, based on stage of life, values, and expectations.

see SPACE

Flexibility:

✓ *Matures*—I've *earned* it. I want time to spend with grandchildren, take more vacations or have time off to test this thing called retirement.

✓ *Boomers*—I *want* it. I want more balance in my life (finally) and flex time to spend with kids, aging parents, grandkids. I want to take my first trip to Europe.

✓ *X-ers*—I *deserve* it. I want flexibility to do the work *my way*. I want to be able to choose between taking that management class or spending the time with friends, family or hobbies.

✓ *Ys*—I *expect* it. I want a sabbatical to live in Japan for a year. I want the freedom to go to lunch with colleagues and come back when we want to.

Do you see the similarities in their wants? They all want something called flexibility. But the differences lie in their assumptions about flexibility. If you understand the nuances, you may be more open to their requests. Managers who can do this will have a tremendous edge over those who can't.

What's a Generation, and Who Are They?

A generation is a group of people who share birth years and therefore share life stages. Generations are defined by spikes and declines in birthrates. The people in those groups are influenced by the cultural events, changes, and challenges that they experience, especially during their formative years. As a result, they bring their own set of attitudes, perceptions, and values to the workplace.

> *"To be part of a generation is much more than the simple matter of your birthday. It's to be a part of an era. It's to have fallen in love with a rock band and not a big band. Or to have played ball with an aluminum bat instead of a wooden one. It's to have done things as no other generation would."*
>
> —Unknown

Today's workplace contains four distinct generations, each bringing its unique perspective and expectations. No wonder we have plenty of opportunities for generation gaps! The birth dates and population of each group varies slightly, depending on whose research you are using. (We used *American Generations: Who They Are, How They Live, What They Think*, by Susan Mitchell.[71]) We suggest you worry less about the generational labels or dates and, instead, ask yourself, "How are they different—or similar? And how can that knowledge help me keep them?"

TO DO . . .

As you read this chapter, ponder these questions. Then discuss them with your team or business unit. Be sure to include representatives from each generation if possible.

- ✓ How is each generation in our work unit unique? What special capabilities does each generation have to contribute?
- ✓ What captures each generation's attention about our work environment?
- ✓ What generations are represented in our current and future customer bases?
- ✓ To be "generation-friendly," what should we stop doing?
- ✓ What can we start doing or increase to be "generation friendly"?

- ✓ What can we do to bridge generational communication in our work environment?
- ✓ What policies, practices, and initiatives should we be looking at through generational "lenses"?[72]

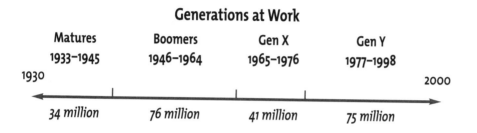

Generations at Work

Matures	Boomers	Gen X	Gen Y
1933–1945	1946–1964	1965–1976	1977–1998

1930   2000

| 34 million | 76 million | 41 million | 75 million |

Generation Y (1977–1998)

Who are the newest members of your workforce? They're the summer interns, recent college grads, and new MBAs. Some are already lawyers, and many are on their second job. They could be your assistant or your boss. There is more curiosity about this group than any other and that makes sense. They haven't been in the workplace long enough for us to know how they will impact it—and us.

In their course "Engaging the Generations," Diane Thielfoldt and Devon Scheef say this about Gen Y:[73]

> *"They call themselves Gen Y. We call them* Generation Y-not?, *because they're packed with power and potential. The challenge for leaders in the future is living up to the high standards and expectations that this generation brings to the workplace. Can we measure up?"*

Gen Ys are also known as the Millennial Generation, the Nexters, and the Echo Boomers. There are 75 million people in this group, and they promise to have as great an impact on the workplace as the similarly sized Boomer generation.

What They Bring and What They Want

Gen Ys are digital natives. They've grown up with cell phones, beepers, and their own e-mail addresses. They not only have PCs; they have servers—to run a second business, if desired. They are great multitaskers. Just watch them do homework while they chat on their cell phones, answer e-mail, watch TV, and surf the Internet. They're hard workers and used to meeting high expectations. They appreciate structure, process, and feedback.

Waving money in the faces of Gen Y as a hiring tool is often a futile effort. What makes a job hot is more about flexibility and freedom than ladder climbing and cold cash. They want the money, but on their own terms: good hours, a good work climate, and a job that offers opportunities to learn and grow.[74] Bottom line: They want *cool*, leading-edge careers that make a difference in the world.

Many prefer group activities to individual pursuits. They're great team players. They are tolerant of authority and diversity and are the best-educated generation in U.S. history. This group is also the best prepared for globalization. They've always had access to world news (CNN was born about the same time they were), they've loved Pokémon cards along with kids from Japan, and they've found a MacDonald's restaurant in every country they've visited.

Gen Ys are civic minded, intellectually curious, and polite. They are not drawn to unstable companies or those with high turnover, and they won't job-hop as often as the X-er. Generational pundits are predicting that this generation will greatly resemble the Matures at work.

Hints for Hanging On

Remember to ask each Gen Y what will keep him or her. Take A through Z into account, but be sure to include these strategies:

✓ *Opportunities*—Find ways for them to exercise their intellectual curiosity and work in teams. They're used to being challenged and structured, so invite them to dive in and co-create their next assignment or promotional opportunity. Be sure to give them the technology they are used to. They're already dependent on it.

✓ **Truth**—Give them regular, honest feedback. They've been raised on schedules, tests, and constant input from tutors, teachers, parents and coaches, all working to build excellence. They want more than the annual performance appraisal.

✓ **Goals**—Help them create stretch goals, multiple career options, and a sense of job security. And remember to reward them when they achieve the goals, in ways that matter most to them (recognition, day off, bonus, latest technology).

Generation X (1965–1976)

Since the first edition of *Love 'Em or Lose 'Em*, this group has grown up. They were the new kids on the block then, and now they're not. We've had a chance to work with them, manage them, and report to them. They're not a mystery anymore.

There are 41 million of them, and they represent almost one-third of the workforce. They are the wellspring of management talent that is expected to take over as the Boomers exit the workplace. And there aren't enough of them to do that job. In fact, the population of workers aged 35–44 will decrease by 15 percent by 2010.[75] X-ers will be stretched thin (yes, even thinner than today), and they'll have multiple options as organizations compete for their talent.

What They Bring and What They Want

When older workers look at an X-er's resumé, they often conclude "a job-hopper." The work history may look fragmented to an older hiring manager but makes perfect sense to the X-er. For X-ers, an organization is a place to learn new skills and build experience, a springboard to a new opportunity there or elsewhere. Many X-ers' resumés reflect this perspective, showing five or six jobs within as many years. When they join you, many of them bring a breadth of experience that will strengthen your team.

Gen-X-ers bring an independent approach to their work. They want to clearly understand what's expected, but once expectations are established and deliverables are defined, they need to have space,

Alas

The pay was good. The location was great. But I knew I could do much more. They wanted me to keep doing what I was doing. So I left.

—X-er in a high-tech company

resources, and the freedom to produce the desired results, in their own way and in their own time.

While the X-ers do not offer "blind" loyalty to a company, they can be fiercely loyal to a project, a team, a boss they like, the mission of the organization, and, yes, even the organization itself. But that loyalty is based on the notion of mutuality. As long as they are challenged, growing, and enjoying the work—and as long as you are getting what you want and need from them—they'll stay. When that partnership weakens or the scales tip to one side, they'll be outta there!

They also want balance between work and their personal lives. They have boundaries, and they use those boundaries effectively. That doesn't mean they won't put in the occasional all-nighter when it's needed. But don't expect they'll do that for the next 20 years. Many feel that one of the greatest gifts of this generation to the rest of us is introducing the expectation of work/life balance. They don't live to work. They work to live.

Hints for Hanging On

Remember to *ask* each X-er what will keep him or her. Take A through Z into account, but be sure to include these strategies:

✓ *Careers*—Keep them challenged and learning. They see your workplace as a stop along the way and a place to build their portfolio of skills and a strong resumé. Help them develop new skills and identify career options in your organization.

✓ *Information*—Keep them in the loop. Communicate early, honestly, and often, in ways that work for them. E-mail is a favorite for this generation, but face-to-face will build the relationship and increase the odds of keeping them.

✓ **Space**—Provide flexibility, freedom, and work/life balance. Do not micromanage these people. Find out what kind of freedom they value most and how they can increase balance in their lives. (If you're from an older generation, take a lesson from them on this one!)

Some readers have said to us, "Wait—I'm a Boomer and I want the same things X-ers want." This is probably true. Here's the difference: If Boomers don't get these things, they'll whine around the water cooler. If X-ers don't get them, they'll walk! While their wants may not differ greatly from those of other employees, X-ers are more willing to say what they want and to leave if you don't deliver.

Baby Boomers (1946–1964)

There are 76 million people in this generation, sometimes divided into two groups: the early Boomers and the late Boomers. "King and Queen of the corporate hill," Boomers are competitive and hardworking. They represent 45 percent of the workforce. Their focus on personal goals and achievement has been the hallmark of their generation. And now, as they reach middle age, Boomers are beginning to question the meaning and purpose of their lives—again. Some are part of the "sandwich generation," raising kids and caring for aging parents at the same time. Others, whose children are grown and gone, have more time on their hands and plenty of disposable income. They're wondering how and when they'll find the time to enjoy it!

What They Bring and What They Want

Boomers have a driven "get it done at all costs" attitude that has made them phenomenally successful. At the same time, that attitude often conflicts with the two younger generations, who see Boomers as having sacrificed everything, including family life, for their own achievement and self-fulfillment. Boomers have been called the "Me" generation and accused of being self-absorbed. On the other hand, they see the attitudes of the two younger generations as an unwillingness to "pay their dues" and "earn their stripes."

Now, they're looking for balance and a way out. They're pondering early retirement, but they don't necessarily intend to stop working. In fact, an AARP survey of 1,500 workers aged 45–75 reported that 70 percent will keep working in retirement.[76] The question is, What kind of work will they be doing if they're no longer working for you?

Hints for Hanging On

Remember to ask each Boomer what will keep him or her. Take A through Z into account, but be sure to include these strategies:

✓ *Passion*—Help them find meaningful work. They've been looking for meaning in their work and lives since they were ten. Ask what they're passionate about, what some of their current interests are, and how they might blend those passions with their work. Ask, too, what new role they might like to play. They have plenty of energy and time left to contribute to your team.

✓ *Enrich*—Keep them on their cutting edge. Teach them. They still want to learn, even the oldest of them. Visit a junior college and notice the silver hair in the world history, pottery, and political science classes. Ask what new thing they'd like to learn this coming year.

✓ *Reward*—Notice and thank them for their dedication and commitment. They're annoyed with the Gen X's and Gen Y's apparent disinterest in loyalty, commitment, and a work-'til-you-drop mentality. They want you to acknowledge those values and characteristics, and if you do, they'll continue to give you their all.

Note: The pending departure of Baby Boomers is such a hot issue, we've added another section on the topic in our Troubleshooting Guide, page 245.

Matures (1933–1945)

They are also known as Veterans, the Swing Generation, the Silents and Pre-Boomers. There are 34 million people in this generation. Rich with work experience, they built many traditional corporations through their hard work and loyalty. They appreciate and understand the importance of achieving common goals and offer a lasting knowledge legacy. With a pending labor shortage, you may want them to stay a little while longer.

What They Bring and What They Want

Matures lead your company, retain your customers, and carry your institutional memories. They are civic minded and helping oriented. And they have a significant knowledge legacy, if only someone will remember to tap into it.

> *In the movie* About Schmidt, *Jack Nicholson sits at his desk, watching the clock tick toward 5 P.M. on his last day of work. He's retiring. His life's work at this company now seems to reside in a pile of boxes in his cleaned out office. He keeps asking people, "When are they coming for the boxes?" Five o'clock comes. It's time for Schmidt to leave his office for the final time. And the boxes sit there. No one came to get them.*

Hints for Hanging On

Remember to ask each Mature what will keep him or her. Take A through Z into account, but be sure to include these strategies:

✓ *Dignity*—Respect and mine their knowledge. Tell them how much you value what they bring to you, the team, and the organization. Then, really *use* what they bring!

✓ *Mentor*—Let them mentor younger workers and pass on their wisdom and knowledge.

> *"The company will be in for a real eye-opening as the older workforce is released. No one is teaching the intangibles of the job. You can teach an employee what a pump is and how it works—but not what it sounds like when it's going bad."*
>
> —Oil company employee[77]

✓ *Link*—Connect them to the community as a way of leveraging their expertise. Ask if they'd like to serve on your organization's community service committee or head up the next charity drive.

And, here's one more . . .

✓ *Hire*—When you start running short on talent, or you want some-one smart, loyal, hardworking, and connected to your customers, consider hiring a Mature. Companies like Toys 'R' Us, The Home Depot, and Anheuser-Busch have recently partnered with AARP to match job-seeking senior workers with the right employers. It's a win-win.[78]

"They realize that 50-plus workers aren't people who wear Depends and complain about their arthritis. We don't think of ourselves as old. We think of ourselves as 40 years old."
—Gary Geyer, 50plusMag.com[79]

Now you have enough theory. Let's try applications.

Clash Avoidance

I hired a young, talented woman with a master's degree in communications. After working for us for just a year, she asked for time off—and not just for a vacation. She asked for a one-year break to take a job as Cinderella in Disneyland, Japan. I talked it over with my boss and we decided to give her an unpaid sabbatical. She is so talented, and we want her back. I feel confident she'll come back and hope she will spend many years working with us.

—Manager, public relations firm

This manager could have considered her request absurd, based on the fact that he (a Boomer) *never* would have asked for a year-long sabbatical after one year with a company. Instead, he took generational differences into account and then valued this employee enough to explore the possibilities with her. Can you do that?

Here are a few other culture clashes we've heard about:

✓ The hiring manager (a Boomer) is interviewing a Gen Y (age 22). When he asks the candidate what questions she might have, she answers, "How much vacation will I get, and when can I take the first one?"

✓ A Gen X-er says no thanks to a "mandatory" training class. He tells his Boomer boss that he plans to use a mentor and read a book on the topic instead.

✓ A Gen Y reports to a Gen X who is an "absentee manager."

✓ An X-er tells his Mature boss that he has to leave to attend his son's soccer match, even though the project isn't done.

✓ A Mature wants to "brief" a Gen Y before she goes to meet a long-time customer. She says, "No, thanks, we'll do fine."

Do these ring a bell for you? How would you stop, think, and avoid a clash, knowing what you now know?

I do not like this person. I must get to know him better.

—Abraham Lincoln

Here's a cheat sheet that might help you remember some of the generational differences. Use it to better engage all members of your workforce!

	Matures	Boomers	Generation X	Generation Y
Work Ethic	Work 'til you drop.	Work long hours, and tell you about it.	Personal life first, work is important.	Lifestyle comes first.
Loyalty	Loyal to employer	Loyal to employer, with reservations	Career and professional loyalty	Career options
Tech-nology	Technology fascination	Technology challenged (40%)	Technology-proficient (80%)	Technology-savvy (100%)
Reporting Relation-ships	Strong chain of command	Chain of command	What is the purpose of a chain of command?	Be respectful but move ahead.

BOTTOM LINE

The challenge of motivating and retaining our multigenerational work-force will continue. Learn about their differences, not to separate them but to understand them better and work with them more effectively. Use A to Z strategies with all, but keep in mind those that appear to matter most to each generation. Notice and leverage the commonalities, too—we're more alike than we are different. And remember that retention is essentially an individual activity. Find out what each of your talented employees wants, regardless of his or her generation.

Chapter 25

YIELD

Power Down

Too bad my boss always needed to be right!

—A.J.

Think about being on a highway on-ramp in a busy city, at an intersection with no stop signs, or in a line forming at the movies. When someone says, "No, *you* go first," with a smile and gesture, you may think how remarkable and rare that action is.

Similarly, in many workplaces, yielding is all too rare. It appears that most managers want to hang on to their power and prestige once they finally have it. In the short term, it may feel great to be so important or powerful, but there will be costs in the long term.

Research and our own experience teach us that when you yield occasionally to your employees, you empower them to think for themselves, to be more creative, more enthusiastic and probably more productive. Your employees' enthusiasm and sense of value as team members will increase the odds that they will stay engaged and stick around.

"Power Down? I Just Got Powered Up!"

A sense of newly found power is one of the joys of being promoted into a leadership role. Even if you were never consciously looking to be more powerful, it may be ego-gratifying to be anointed as skilled enough to make bigger decisions, direct others' activities, and even take the spotlight bows for team successes.

Once you receive that kind of power, it might be difficult to give some away. Many of our role models taught us to hang on to that power—to wield it fairly (the benevolent dictator type)—but never to give it away. Then management books in the 1980s proclaimed empowerment, and with it came confusion for many managers, who asked, "Why should I let my employees make more decisions, take more credit, be in charge? And once you tell me why, tell me how to empower my people."

So let's take a look at these two critical questions: Why yield and how can you yield?

Why Yield? What's in It for You?

This case study highlights several benefits of yielding.

Alas

A manager in a leading drug research and development company (we'll call her Joan) woke up one morning and recognized that 20 percent of her employees were doing 80 percent of the thinking. She was concerned for a number of reasons:

✓ *The 80 percent of her employees who weren't really using their creative and intellectual abilities also seemed to be disengaged or just going through the motions at work. Their job satisfaction level seemed low, and in many cases she knew they could be more productive if they were more involved somehow in the work.*

✓ *The competition would gain an edge if her company didn't use talent better, get more creative, and stay on the cutting edge.*

(continued)

> ✓ She and a handful of thinking employees were overstretched and spent much of their time answering questions and meeting with others to solve their problems.
> ✓ She had lost some talented employees and learned in the exit interviews that they were not being challenged enough and had grown bored.
>
> *What is wrong with this picture?*

Joan knew the following:

✓ She needed to leverage the brilliance and creativity in her group.
✓ She needed to get people more engaged in their work.
✓ She needed to increase job satisfaction and all the benefits connected to it (like productivity).
✓ She needed to free up her time—and that of some of her other *thinking* employees—spent answering questions and making decisions for others.
✓ She needed to retain her talent!

Joan knew she had to do something to meet these goals. It took her a while to realize that her solution was right in front of her all the time. We'll look at what Joan did to solve her problem in a minute. For now, look at your situation.

TO DO . . .

Check out this list:

✓ Is your organization lean and mean, like so many others after years of downsizing?
✓ Is your span of control larger than ever and are the expectations from above constantly increasing your workload and pressure?

see OPPORTUNITIES

✓ Do some of your employees seem apathetic or less than eager to show up on Monday mornings?

✓ Are many of your employees still waiting to be told what to do every step of the way?

✓ Is the competition nipping at your heels?

✓ Have you lost any of your talented team members because they were bored or needed a new challenge?

If your answers are no, then either you are already yielding power to your employees or you aren't yet feeling the pressure to do so. If that's the case, move on to another chapter to focus on something that matters more right now or that you may not already be doing quite as well.

If you answered yes to four or more on the checklist, then read on. You have just identified the reasons to power down. You must yield to your people in order to compete successfully. And you must yield in order to keep your talented employees on your team.

> *"The higher up you go in an organization, the more you need to let other people be the winners and not make it all about winning yourself. For bosses, that means being careful about how you hand out encouragement. If you find yourself saying, 'Great ideas, but . . . ,' try cutting your response off at 'idea.'"*
> —Marshall Goldsmith, Executive Coach[80]

Who's Got the Right of Way?

You may be convinced that you could benefit by giving more power to your employees, yet find it difficult to know where to start. The rules can be fuzzy or hard to remember, just like the road rules that guide merging onto a busy highway or crossing an intersection that has no stop signs.

In the matter of powering down to your employees, the uncertainty is even greater because *there are no rules.* Your organization establishes cultural norms and role models, but as an individual manager you have tremendous leeway to give power.

Let's take another look at the case study to see how Joan yielded.

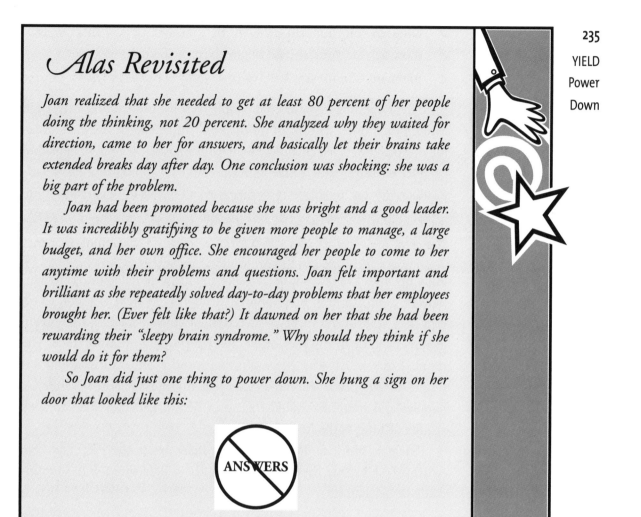

Alas Revisited

Joan realized that she needed to get at least 80 percent of her people doing the thinking, not 20 percent. She analyzed why they waited for direction, came to her for answers, and basically let their brains take extended breaks day after day. One conclusion was shocking: she was a big part of the problem.

Joan had been promoted because she was bright and a good leader. It was incredibly gratifying to be given more people to manage, a large budget, and her own office. She encouraged her people to come to her anytime with their problems and questions. Joan felt important and brilliant as she repeatedly solved day-to-day problems that her employees brought her. (Ever felt like that?) It dawned on her that she had been rewarding their "sleepy brain syndrome." Why should they think if she would do it for them?

So Joan did just one thing to power down. She hung a sign on her door that looked like this:

What? That's it? End of story? Well, yes, basically. Joan explained to her employees that she had been underserving and undervaluing them by answering all of their questions and giving them step-by-step direction. She admitted to them that she had also robbed the organization of tremendous intellectual and creative capital by giving answers instead of asking questions. So when people came through her open door and asked their questions as they always had, she pointed to the sign and asked them powerful, thought-provoking questions like these:

✓ What do you think the problem is?

✓ Who do you think should be involved in solving this issue?

✓ What are the choices we have?

These questions empowered people to solve problems creatively, to lean on each other instead of on the boss, and to come up with multiple options. She gave encouragement and praise as people struggled to produce outstanding, creative solutions and new approaches. Her team's productivity and retention rates surpassed all others in the organization. Other managers came to her to find out what she was doing to magically inspire such phenomenal results.

Joan chuckled as she related the secret of her success. "I had to set aside my ego. I could not be the all-knowing sage if I wanted my employees' brains to keep functioning. I truly had to yield to them, to accept them as brilliant, eager-to-succeed colleagues. I had to power down, give them some of my previously guarded power and importance. The result is that we all win. My job is easier and more gratifying and our results are the best ever. The best part is my most talented people are happier and more motivated than ever before and they plan to stick around as long as the fun continues."

There is more to Joan's approach than meets the eye. The "No Answers" sign could be an annoyance if the follow-through did not include key elements:

✓ ***Trust your employees to come up with the answers.*** Even if you would have done it another way, consider the approaches they create and support them all the way.

> *A manager at Kraft Foods yielded to his assembly-line workers. They developed a schedule and a new team system that boosted production, reduced overhead costs and downtime, and improved recruitment and retention.*

✓ ***Manage your reactions when you yield and they crash!*** Powering down and yielding are sometimes risky and there will be failures. Instead of punishing, collaborate with your empowered employees to learn from the mistake. Focus on what they could do differently next time around, rather than the rearview mirror approach of what they should have done.

A senior manager made a mistake that cost his company $10 million. As he walked into his boss's office, he anticipated anger and most probably a firing. His boss asked him what he had learned from the mistake, and he quickly listed all the things he would do differently next time. Then he waited for the ax to fall. And he waited. Finally, he asked, "Aren't you going to fire me?" The boss answered, "Why would I fire you? I just invested $10 million in your learning."

✓ ***Serve your employees.*** Be a resource to them. To yield doesn't mean you take the next exit. Empowerment spells disaster in too many cases where the manager tosses decisions and workloads at his employees and then moves on to bigger things. The "No Answers" approach works only if you are willing to brainstorm with them when they are stumped, and to give them guidance and feedback along the way.

✓ ***See them as colleagues more often than as subordinates.*** Show it by occasionally doing work that may seem "beneath you."

A Southwest Airlines pilot was chatting with a young couple with a baby in the front seat of the airplane. The luggage was being loaded when the young mother realized that the baby's bottle was in the checked luggage, not the carry-on bag. She looked frantically out the window and spotted the blue suitcase. The pilot asked which one was theirs and then scrambled down the stairs onto the tarmac to retrieve the bottle. The young woman and the pilot exchanged signals while he found the suitcase, opened it, and found the bottle. As he entered the plane with the prize, the flight attendants and passengers who had been watching burst into applause. He could have asked a flight attendant to do it, but think what he gained by yielding, by powering down, and just doing it himself.

✓ ***Give the spotlight away.*** This may be the toughest of all. As the hero, you may have received the applause from your employees and they may have credited you with the team's success. Powering down means sharing the stage and the applause with your team members. Ironically, your stock will go up with your employees as you increasingly give them room to perform (and get credit for) brilliant, creative work.

Nordstrom managers yield by letting employees practice what the employee handbook preaches: "Use your own best judgment at all times." A manager told the story of her employee returning late from a lunch break, out of breath. When asked why she was out of breath (not why she was late), the employee responded, "A pregnant customer ordered a new bathrobe and it just came in. When I called to tell her about it, I found out she went to the hospital this morning to give birth, so I decided to use my lunch break and run it over to her." The customer wrote an appreciation letter to Nordstrom's senior management, and the employee was recognized and rewarded for her outstanding customer service.

Do you ever see that kind of customer service in a tightly controlled, micromanaged environment? Probably not. And count on it: empowered employees will have great ideas or take on tasks you may not have asked them to perform. They will put their own signatures on excellence. They may even take your breath away.

BOTTOM LINE

Yielding will increase the odds of retaining your best people. As you give people more power to create, make decisions, and truly affect the success of the team, their job satisfaction (and your odds of keeping them) will go up. At the same time, your ability to compete successfully and accomplish your business goals will increase. You have phenomenal power to yield. Try it and see what happens.

Chapter 26

ZENITH

Go for It

One of my best employees gave notice yesterday. And I thought I knew all there was to know about retaining key people! I'm determined to create a place where this is not the norm.

—A.J.

You've done it. You're at Z. You may have come here through any number of routes. Some of you diligently read each of the chapters in this book. Others have skimmed, scanned, and landed here. Others came immediately to Z because they like to read the last first.

Whichever path brought you here, we have a series of questions for you to answer. If you have read all the chapters or even skimmed them, these questions will show you how much you've absorbed and what work you may still need to do. If you start here, this inventory will direct you to the specific chapters you may want to read first. In any case, this self-test is for you.

Each question addresses the main theme of that chapter (A to Z). We ask you to be honest and to ask yourself if you (still?) hold these beliefs about managing others. (Note: It is impossible to end up with a *no* for all of the 26 questions.)

What's Your REI?
Retention/Engagement Index: A Manager's Self-Test

Do you ...

	Yes	No		If you checked yes, read:
A.	☐	☐	Assume that employees will tell you what they want from their work?	ASK
B.	☐	☐	Believe that retention is a job for HR or compensation professionals?	BUCK
C.	☐	☐	Regard employees' careers as their business, not yours?	CAREERS
D.	☐	☐	Take for granted that employees know you respect them, and therefore you don't need to show it?	DIGNITY
E.	☐	☐	Think employees should tell you if they are not feeling challenged in their work?	ENRICH
F.	☐	☐	Expect employees to leave their personal lives at the door and feel only their business life is your concern?	FAMILY
G.	☐	☐	Avoid discussing career options with employees, especially when promotions are not readily available?	GOALS
H.	☐	☐	Hire primarily based on functional or technical skills?	HIRE
I.	☐	☐	Give information to employees on a need-to-know basis only?	INFORMATION
J.	☐	☐	Feel you are here to get the job done, that employees don't have to like you?	JERK
K.	☐	☐	Believe you are not at work to have fun?	KICKS
L.	☐	☐	Fear that if you introduce employees to others in your network, they might be enticed away?	LINK
M.	☐	☐	Feel that you don't have time to mentor?	MENTOR
N.	☐	☐	Have only a vague idea of what it costs to lose talented people?	NUMBERS
O.	☐	☐	Tend to hoard good people instead of helping them seek other opportunities?	OPPORTUNITIES
P.	☐	☐	Agree that we don't have the luxury of loving what we do?	PASSION
Q.	☐	☐	Fail to question policies for the sake of your employees?	QUESTION

	Do you . . .			If you checked yes, read:
	Yes	No		
R.	☐	☐	Deem good work to be its own reward?	REWARD
S.	☐	☐	Feel that if you don't control the who, how, where, and when, the work won't get done right?	SPACE
T.	☐	☐	Avoid giving negative or corrective feedback to your employees?	TRUTH
U.	☐	☐	Consider yourself too busy to be a good listener?	UNDERSTANDING
V.	☐	☐	View employees' values as their own business and therefore seldom discuss them?	VALUES
W.	☐	☐	Believe that employee health programs and initiatives are frills?	WELLNESS
X.	☐	☐	Think that generational differences are irrelevant in the workplace?	X-ERS & OTHER GENERATIONS
Y.	☐	☐	Believe employees should usually wait for you to tell them what to do?	YIELD
Z.	☐	☐	Maintain that employee engagement and retention are not critical leadership skills and you don't need to spend time improving them?	ZENITH

So, how do you score? Here is how to make sense of the test and decide what to do next.

TO DO . . .

✓ *Score the REI.* If your no's outnumber your yes's, you're on the right track. If your yes's far outnumber your no's, you've got work to do. Highlight the yes's and turn to those chapters. Read (or reread) them and look for just one or two strategies to try in your own work group. Work, focus, and have patience. It takes at least three weeks to develop a new habit.

I realized that in general I have created a pretty good retention culture. But as open as I thought I was, I also see that I need to work on

giving people more space—space to do the work in their own way, as long as they get the results, and even some space to flex their work hours whenever possible. That's my focus for the next few months.
—Team leader, manufacturing organization

✓ ***Get feedback.*** As you try something new, it may feel strange. Ask your trusted employees or colleagues to tell you what's working and what's not.

I decided that I need to show people that I care about them and respect the work that they do for me. At first, when I wandered into their work areas just to ask how things were going, they nervously looked at me, waiting for some criticism or concern. After a few weeks, though, they warmed up. I asked for feedback, and one of the more vocal employees told me that he and others have noticed the change in my behavior and they really appreciate it. That positive input keeps me going.
—Manager, engineering firm

✓ ***Reward yourself and choose again.*** Acknowledge your success. Give yourself the praise you deserve. Then choose another strategy to work on.

I've worked on mentoring and have definitely improved. I've patted myself on the back, and my employees' reactions to me are an even greater reward. Next, I'm taking on fun. We have been all work, no play for too long. I think I'll start the ball rolling by ordering pizza this Friday afternoon and turning off the phones. I plan to just chat with my team about how we can enjoy work more. I'm sure they'll have some great ideas.
—Owner, executive search firm

Calling All Managers of Managers

How can we deliver world-class service without world-class people?
—Fred Smith, CEO, Federal Express

If you manage other managers, you'll want to send them a clear message about their responsibility to keep talented people. You will want to clearly define retention goals, accountability, and consequences for reaching (or missing) those goals. Think about the message you send to the managers who report to you. Here is an example of one leader's message:

see BUCK

> *The key now is to continue to execute better than anyone else in the industry. I've seen you operate. I know how well you can execute. And I'm confident that you can not only meet the goals your management has set but exceed them. Of course, there are two keys to superb execution. Great management is one. But the other is great people. And today, great people are hard to find. So when we find talented employees, we simply cannot afford to lose them.*
>
> *Along with your regular sales and service goals, I want you to make talent retention a top priority. Remember: No one plays a more important role in talent retention than you. In the eyes of our employees, you are the company. The culture you create in your department—the personal rewards and respect you provide, the time you take to understand and coach each individual on your staff— these are the keys to retaining and motivating our people. We hold each of you accountable for developing and motivating your people. That's what will make us thrive.*
>
> —Lon A. Smith, past president and CEO, Hartford Life

TO DO . . .

Beyond sending your message to managers, try this: Meet with your fellow leaders to discuss the questions here. Dialogue about your different approaches. Agree. Act. Evaluate. Continue.

Key Questions

✓ How will we compete for talent differently?

✓ What will we do about the "jerks" who report to us (those managers who don't treat their people well)?

✓ How will we see that the *Love 'Em* philosophy cascades down?

✓ How will we give our managers incentive to think beyond pay and perks to keep their talent?

✓ How will we reward managers for taking risks to engage and retain talent?

✓ How will we hold managers accountable for retention planning?

✓ How will we help others broaden their sense of who belongs in the "star" category?

✓ How will we support the continual training of our reporting managers in these retention strategies?

✓ How will we bring these ideas to the attention of those senior to us? How will we influence them to take action?

✓ How will we know if we are successful? What are the goals for our business units? How will we sustain this initiative?

The Zenith—The Best

We worked with an organization that believed in holding what senior managers called "zenith" meetings—where three or four teams of people were brought together to discuss and ultimately agree on high level goals and strategies to help them reach those goals. The idea is to reach higher than ever before, to continually improve and stretch, as individuals and as an organization. At these meetings you ask each other, "Could we do better?" "Could we stretch higher?" And you don't stop when you find the zenith, the high point. You simply keep at it.

We hope you will keep at it. Evaluate yourself often and commit to improving continuously. Hold yourself and the managers who report to you accountable for building a workplace so productive and fulfilling that your talented people will want to stay, create, and make their mark. That's the Zenith.

We wish you well.

—Bev and Sharon

P. S. Please write and tell us what happened at www.keepem.com.

TROUBLESHOOTING GUIDE

More Ways to Win the Talent War

- They *quit quickly!* We barely get them hired and trained and they leave us—for something "better."
- The boomers might be *bailing out.* How do I keep them a little longer?
- They have the *workplace blues.* How do I light the fire again?
- *What about them?* I wish they would ask *directly* for what they want.

What keeps you awake at night?

Wondering how to keep good people—and keep them engaged—*should* keep you from sleeping through the Talent War.

Why add this guide? Because some troubles just don't fit in one particular chapter, or they cut across several. These are timely concerns and pressing problems that we've heard from managers, the media, and senior leaders of organizations large and small, representing virtually all industries around the globe. Every issue relates to winning the Talent War.

When you can do a good job with troubles like these, you'll win. Good people, who now have multiple options, will choose to work for you!

Go up against these questions to test your ability to engage and retain your good people.

QUICK QUITS

You recruit. You hire. You train. Within a year, they leave. Managers we talk to often vent their deep frustration with the loss of talent within the first year of employment. Recruiters are frustrated, too. No one wants to spend time and dollars finding the right people, only to have to start all over again.

Q: I recently hired someone who left within the first quarter. He never gave this organization (or me) a chance. I never even knew he was unhappy. It makes me angry. We spent good money recruiting him, and I invested time training him. How do I prevent this next time?

Both you and your recruiter (and others who sat in on the interviews and checked references) thought the fit was right. But something changed, or something didn't happen!

We believe that many quick quits *can* be prevented. We think that there is a direct correlation between that shortened tenure and actions you take. (Yup, sorry, *you* again.)

We believe that most new hires come into an organization excited about their new adventure and filled with energy and potential. Too many managers admit that they leave the "get to know you" stuff to their organization's orientation program. Yes, they meet with their new hires, introduce them around, and then, well, the connection seems to die. You can't let that happen.

One of the authors met with a group of new recruits in a very well-respected "destination" high-tech organization, one that hired all those smart, savvy, innovative Gen Y's. The recruiting was easy. The stay factor was difficult.

One new recruit spoke for all of them:

"I think they thought that because I was at the top of my class, or a high-potential in my previous organization, I could learn the ropes easily in this new place. The truth was, I couldn't. It was harder than I thought to break in. After the orientation period, I was left totally on my own."

So they're left on their own. What can go wrong? They can have a major disconnect, that's what. They can disconnect with

✓ you or their coworkers,
✓ the job itself, or
✓ the organization (work environment, norms, or values).

You can prevent all three types of disconnects by taking a few preventive steps. You'll notice that each step requires chatting with that new employee often, asking powerful questions and providing support in every way you can.

Connect to You and to Coworkers

There is no better way to predict retention and engagement than to assess the links that new hires establish with their manager and colleagues. Don't assume they want to go to lunch with the team every day, but don't assume they want to eat alone. Find out what works best for them, but be certain they begin to connect (in their own way) with you and their colleagues. In your early, ongoing conversations, you might ask questions like these:

✓ How are you getting along with your other team members? Are there introductions to other colleagues you'd like me to make?
✓ So far, what leads you to believe that you've made the right choice in accepting this job? Is there anything that might lead you to question your choice?
✓ What will it take to keep your energy? What do you need to stay interested and involved in the team?
✓ What do you need me to do more of, less of? How can I support you as you get acclimated?

Connect to the Job

They joined your organization because you offered work they love to do. Are they doing it? Or is there a disconnect? Find out if the job measures up to what you promised. If it doesn't, find ways to close the gap. Ask questions like these to be sure your new talent is doing the work they love:

✓ How does the job measure up to what we promised so far? Where are we on or off? How might we course-correct?
✓ What other interests would you like to explore, either now or over time?
✓ What do you find most challenging about the job? What is not challenging enough about it?
✓ How can I help you fine-tune this job over time?

Connect to the Organization (Environment, Norms, Values)

Your new recruits may or may not have carefully evaluated your organization before they committed. In fact, it's tough to do during the interview process. The job sounded great, you seemed like a good manager, and the people were nice. Now they're on board. No one told them you all work 60-hour weeks. You forgot to mention how competitive this place is and that there's been a lot of turmoil around here lately. One month into the job, they're wondering who or what they joined. Are their values and yours compatible? 🔲 Early on, ask questions like these:

✓ What have you learned about our organization that surprises you (either good or not so good)?
✓ How does the work pace and schedule work for you? Is there anything we need to adjust?
✓ How is our organization the same or different from your last employer? What do you miss most? Least?
✓ How can I help you get more of what you want from this workplace? We want you to be happy here!

Yes, all this conversation and connecting requires time and energy on your part. But think about the goal: preventing a quick quit.

BOOMER BAILOUT

Look at the facts. Run the numbers. You'll see you might, indeed, have a problem. Baby Boomers represent 60 percent of the workforce aged 25–54, and every 7 seconds another one turns 50. One half of them will be eligible to retire in the next decade, and there simply aren't enough skilled workers to replace them.[81]

Q: Everyplace I look, I read that the Baby Boomers are approaching retirement and that organizations are going to suffer when they leave. In fact, I hear rumors every week in my own department about someone else in that age group taking an early retirement. Is that something I should be worried about? Do something about?

Worry? Not good for your health. It is important, however, to consider your own situation and then figure out what to do and when to do it. Demographics alone predict an employee marketplace. That means that for many managers, the problem isn't just one of filling the hole left by a departing star. It's filling far too many holes at one time. At an average replacement cost of twice a departing employee's annual salary, imagine the drain on your operating budget and impact on the bottom line if that happens to you.

Some questions to ponder:

✓ What's happening in *your* backyard? Do you anticipate talent shortages caused by Boomer departure or for any other reason?

✓ If your talented Boomers are going to work a while longer, why not keep them in your organization, rather than lose them to the competition?

✓ What will be lost to your organization when they leave?
- Deep knowledge about the business, technology, or organizational culture?
- Wisdom, mentoring ability, wonderful customer relations?

Page 250

- Unwavering dedication and commitment to the job?
- Proven leadership skill and experience?

Based on your answers to the questions, you may decide you want to keep your talented Boomers a while longer. Where and how do you start? There are things you can do as their manager, even if no one else in the organization blesses it. Here are a few for starters:

Sit with every one of these unique individuals, and *ask* what will keep them a while longer. Ask what they want to learn or do next. Listen to their answers and customize your retention strategies, just as you would for a talented worker of any age. Don't assume that just because they're older, they're not learning or growing. In fact, our research shows that the top three reasons workers over 50 stay in their organizations are

- Exciting work, challenge;
- Great people;
- Career growth, learning and development.

Would you have known?

Give Boomers *space*. Be flexible and creative as you brainstorm possibilities with them. If they're leaning toward retirement but aren't sure, consider some ways they might "try before they buy." For example, could they work from home a few days a week or serve your team part-time? Could they shift their working hours to allow time for education, family, or hobbies? Would an extended vacation (sabbatical) help them "test-drive" retirement?

Think about how they could *mentor* others in the organization (one great way to transfer knowledge), and consider challenging projects, learning options, or leadership roles they might want to take on.

Be willing to *question* the long-standing rules in your organization, too. Use your influence skills and run your ideas up the chain of approval if need be.

Baptist Health South Florida, a health care organization, has received numerous awards and recognition as a great place to work. In part, it's because managers at all levels ask the question "How can we keep our older workers a little while longer?" The creative solutions seem endless and include the following:

- *Appoint representatives to help Boomers change jobs internally, such as to less physically demanding jobs or a new challenge.*
- *Provide advanced warning of job displacement, career counselors, scholarships, and tuition assistance.*
- *Offer fitness rooms, wellness programs, disease management, healthy meals, ergonomics support, and life-threatening illness policy.*
- *Suggest phased retirement—employees can draw from the defined-contribution retirement plans at 59 1/2. Some older workers use this policy to reduce their work hours while using their retirement savings to keep a steady salary.*
- *Allow workers to accrue up to 1,000 hours of paid time off, which some use as extended vacations to see if they want that much free time.*[82]

While the Baptist Health story is more about what an entire organization can do to keep Boomers than what one manager can do, every strategy started with one manager's creative contribution and the courage to recommend it (even push it) to decision makers.

We touched on Boomers in the "X-ers and Other Generations" chapter. We stress it again here because we do believe keeping Boomers will help you fight the current Talent War. Many organizations and individual managers are already getting creative with this topic. Why? Because they believe the numbers. So do we.

———————————————————————

WORKPLACE BLUES

It's midway through the decade, and many managers must lead a demoralized, postdownsizing, do-more-with-less workforce. How's your team doing? Are your people disillusioned, disengaged, distrustful, or dissatisfied?

If so, you're not alone. Recent research showed that 70 percent of U.S. workers are either not engaged or are actively disengaged (undermining their engaged coworkers' efforts). That less-than-thrilled feeling is costing the American economy up to $350 billion per year in lost productivity.[83] Eight out of ten workers are expected to jump ship when the economy's lights come back on.[84] They're spending time updating their resumés and logging onto monster.com.

Q: I can't say I was surprised when I read the results of our recent satisfaction surveys. Our employees are more demoralized and disengaged than ever. It's no wonder, after four years of downsizing and belt tightening. Many have been doing the job of two or three workers—and without any additional compensation. I'm afraid that as the options outside open up again, we'll lose some great talent. I'm worried that those losses will affect my department. Can I do anything to light the fire in them again?

Yes, you can. And you can keep them. There is an art and a science to hanging onto and engaging "survivors" of downsizing, right-sizing, mergers/acquisitions, or business downturns. Many of you learned that in the early and mid-1990s when you faced a similar task.

First, recognize how much power and influence you have, as a manager, over engaging your talented people. Research studies tell us that 50 percent of work satisfaction is determined by the relationship workers have with their bosses.[85] They look to you for leadership. They look to you to mentor and to care about them. And on the heels of big changes and tough times, employees look to you for support, communication, and structure. Here is what we mean.

Support

✓ **Open your door.** For months now, you may have been less available than before. You've had more meetings and fewer answers and the result is a closed door. Your employees want (and deserve) access to you.

✓ **Allow grieving.** For many, everything has changed. Coworkers have been laid off, new leadership arrived, and the sign on the door is new. Additionally, many have been working harder than ever before as they make up for the friends that left. Your employees (like you) deserve to whine a bit and to experience the normal feelings of loss.

✓ **Actively listen.** How *are* your listening skills? 🖼 Now is the time to sharpen them. Allow your treasured talent to vent, complain about their exhaustion, tell you what they need and want. If they don't bring it up, ask how they're doing and what they need.

✓ **Do something.** Get them resources. They've done so much with so little for so long. They will love you for getting them the new laptop or hiring a temporary worker to help out on the latest project.

✓ **Celebrate small successes.** How long has it been since you've sprung for pizza for your team, just to say thanks for work well done? Do it.

Communication

✓ **Communicate often and honestly.** 🖼 Yes, you need to do that all the time. But it's especially important during and following tough times, when employees are down and disheartened. As soon as you have the okay to share information, do it. 🖼

✓ **Create new communication channels.** The best approach is still face-to-face. And it's so rare these days that it packs an even more powerful punch. If you don't typically use videos or "all-hands" meetings, they could be a novel and effective approach.

✓ **Communicate vision and direction.** This is tough, but it is so important. First decipher what the vision and direction are. If you can't communicate that for the entire organization, do it for your division, department, or team.

✓ *Seek input from your employees.* They have good ideas. Don't you need those? And remember how valued you feel when someone asks what you think and then listens to your ideas?

Structure

✓ *Provide clear direction.* This means going beyond the communicated vision to provide a detailed road map. Even independent, autonomous employees want to know what you expect from them and how you want them to proceed, day to day.

✓ *Create "winter rules."* In golf, when conditions are not normal, people play by winter rules. They get to tee up the ball in a new place or toss it out of a puddle and into the fairway, all to gain advantage and improve results. Do the same with your team, creating temporary policies, procedures, or reporting relationships to get you through uncertain or tough times.

✓ *Model new behaviors.* If you want an upbeat, focused, positive team, you'll need to act upbeat, focused, and positive. They watch you. They listen to you. When you radiate doom and gloom, they're affected. And when you're excited or optimistic about the team, the organization or the future, they catch that optimism. Tell them what you know about the future and be honest about what you don't.

Research shows that engaged employees are more likely to stay with you, produce more and increase your customers' satisfaction.[86] All of that makes your job easier and improves the bottom line. Offer up an additional dose of support, communication, and structure. You can light the fire again.

WHAT ABOUT THEM?

When we tell managers, "The buck ⏹B stops with you," we often hear, "What about them? I thought people were in charge of their own careers and workplace satisfaction." Managers wonder if engagement and retention have to rest entirely on their shoulders. Here's how one manager put it:

Q: Okay, your reminders and tips are good. But I wonder where my responsibility starts and stops. They think I can read their minds. I don't always know what they want and I'm not sure I always should have to be the one to ask. How can I help them take charge of their own satisfaction?

Good question, frequently asked. We decided to answer it by writing another book, to help employees get more of what they want, without jumping ship or disengaging. *Love It, Don't Leave It: 26 Ways to Get What You Want at Work* takes some of the burden for workplace satisfaction off the manager and places it squarely on employees' shoulders. Here are three examples of the kinds of tips, strategies, and "to-dos" you'll find in *Love It*.

Help Them Assess

Want to get started? Complete this questionnaire yourself and share it with your direct reports. Then, in one-on-one meetings, talk about what each of you has or hasn't done recently. Talk about actions you *and they* could take to increase workplace satisfaction.

✓ I've carefully evaluated and listed (in detail)   (YES/NO)
   what I love about work and what I don't.

✓ I've looked at my latest performance review   (YES/NO)
   and identified a step I could take to improve.

✓ I've chatted with a sympathetic (smart) partner   (YES/NO)
about work and what I want from it.

✓ I've clearly evaluated my role in a workplace   (YES/NO)
dilemma or dissatisfaction.

✓ I've explored and then listed *all* of my options.   (YES/NO)

✓ I've identified what is possible and what isn't,   (YES/NO)
given this organization's culture, leadership, or rules.

✓ I've taken a risk and *talked* to people who might   (YES/NO)
be able to help me.

✓ I've *tried* something new.   (YES/NO)

Help Them Ask

Countless employees say they would rather quit their jobs than ask for what they want. What if you could give them a handy guide to asking? Maybe then they would ask *you*, rather than leave when they're not getting what they want and need. Here are a few tips from the "guide to asking." Share it with your employees.

✓ ***Consider who, when, and how you'll ask.*** Is it the boss who holds the key to your request? Is Friday afternoon a good time to ask? Is it best to ask in person, by e-mail, or on the phone?

✓ ***Identify the barriers and think about the "work-arounds."*** What's in the way of your getting what you want? Create a list of possible ways to overcome those barriers.

✓ ***Find a WIIFT (What's In It For Them?).*** Do not go asking until you can think of at least one benefit for your request grantor. Will you be more productive or engaged if he says yes? Will customers or team members benefit? Will you save time or money? You get the idea.

One boss we know told his employees he *really* wanted them to ask him for whatever they wanted. He promised to listen carefully, consider their requests, and brainstorm the best possible solutions with them. One employee did just that.

My job EKG had gone flat and I was thinking about leaving my company. I decided to take my boss at his word first, though, and arranged a time to talk to him about my situation. After a two-hour talk, we came to an agreement that has completely changed my perspective on work. It was the WIFFT that did it. When I explained how a change in my role could benefit him and the team, he thought about it, we talked about it—and then, he agreed. I'm so glad I asked, rather than jump ship.

If you fail to encourage it, many of your good people will fail to ask. They will simply move on.

Help Them Team

There is tremendous power in teaming. Consider how you might create employee teams to increase job satisfaction, engagement, and retention.

When a manager realized that his team of call center agents had a 46 percent turnover rate as compared to the company's overall rate of 32 percent, he decided to try teaming. He organized three-person teams, provided resources (including *Love It, Don't Leave It*), and gave them an opportunity to work together on their own issues of workplace satisfaction. While the manager worried it would end up as a "gripe" session, he was surprised by the results. Here are four stories he told us:

One team of three represented three different generations (ages 21, 31, 41). In their meetings, they talked about how they were different, made suggestions to one another, and improved relationships and communication across the age gaps.

*****

One team met more than 15 times during the four months, both formally and informally. Initially, they spent a lot of time venting and complaining, but they learned to take that to a new level of problem solving. They developed not only a working relationship but a friendship as well. They used the time to coach each other and problem-solve customer issues and "collection" challenges.

*****

One team member used the team to help her manage home life. She was having trouble juggling all her responsibilities, used the team as a sounding board, and was able to be more productive and manage her time better.

*****

One team convinced a member to stay when he wanted to quit. They suggested he talk to his boss and ask for a change in his work responsibilities. That team saved a great employee for the organization.

In a perfect world, managers and employees would co-create an engaged, productive workforce. Your *real-world* employees may need your prompting to play their roles powerfully. Use these ideas to empower and educate your employees. (Use them to increase your own satisfaction, too!)

And, while you're at it, pick up a copy of *Love It, Don't Leave It: 26 Ways to Get What You Want at Work.*

These aren't the only hot issues we heard about, but they were mentioned so often that we chose to highlight them. We want to hear about *your* troubles. What are your most challenging engagement or retention dilemmas? Write us at www.keepem.com. Thanks!

Notes

1. See www.gallupjournal.com/CA/ee/20020603.asp.
2. See www.bls.gov/emp.
3. Frederick Herzberg, B. Mausner, and B. Snyderman, *The Motivation to Work* (New York: Wiley, 1959).
4. D. Michael Abrashoff, "Retention through Redemption," *Harvard Business Review* (February 2001): 137–141.
5. Marie Gendron, "Keys to Retaining Your Best Managers in a Tight Job Market," *Harvard Management Update* (June 1998): 1–4.
6. Hay Group, "1998–1999 Employee Attitudes Study," *HR/OD* 8 (1 December 1998); "Why Workers Quit," *Arizona Republic*, 26 July 1998; and "Money Can't Buy Employee Commitment, WFD Research Reveals," *Business Wire*, 4 August 1998.
7. Saratoga Institute, "Study of the Emerging Workforce," Interim Services, Inc., Santa Clara, Calif., 1997.
8. Kevin Dobbs, "Knowing How to Keep Your Best and Brightest," *Workforce* 8, no. 4A (1 April 2001).
9. Ibid.
10. Corporate Leadership Council Employee Preferences Database, Corporate Leadership Council research and analysis, Corporate Executive Board, 1998.
11. See www.bls.gov/emp.
12. Adapted from "CareerPower: An Individual Guide to Career Planning," Career Systems International, Inc., Scranton, Pa., 1998.
13. R. Roosevelt Thomas Jr., *Beyond Race and Gender: Unleashing the Power of Your Total Workforce by Managing Diversity* (New York: Amacom, 1991).
14. 2001 Randstad North American Employee Review, Atlanta, Ga., 1-877-922-2468.
15. Pamela Kruger, "Jobs for Life," *Fast Company* (May 2000): 236.

16. Lisa McLaughlin, "In Brief: Elder-Care Stresses," *Time* (19 April 2001): 83.

17. Adapted from "The Decision Grid," The Jordan Evans Group, Cambria, Calif., and Career Systems International, Scranton, Pa., 1997.

18. A report titled "MBA Graduates Want to Work for Caring and Ethical Employers" as found in the Institute for Global Ethics, *Ethics Newsline*, 2 August 2004.

19. JEDlet.com Journal, 12 September 2003.

20. "StartingPower: Re-Recruiting Your Talent in That First Year," Career Systems International, Scranton, Pa., 2001.

21. Sandar Larkin and P. J. Larkin, *Communicating Change: How to Win Employee Support for New Business Directions* (New York: McGraw-Hill, 1994), 14–15.

22. Jack Stack (with Bo Burlingham), *The Great Game of Business* (New York: Currency/ Doubleday, 1994).

23. Joyce M. Rosenberg, "Wise Employers Keep Employees Informed," *Miami Herald*, 16 August 2004.

24. Saratoga Institute, Santa Clara, Calif., 2000.

25. For more information, see "Retention Deficit Disorder," Career Systems International, Scranton, Pa., 2001.

26. Warren Bennis, "News Analysis: It's the Culture," *Fast Company* (August 2003).

27. David Dorsey, "Andy Pearson Finds Love," *Fast Company* (August 2001): 78.

28. David Granirer, "Fun and the Bottom Line: Using Humor to Retain Employees," *About HR*, 2 April 2003.

29. Saratoga Institute, "Study of the Emerging Workforce."

30. Dave Hemsath and Leslie Yerkes, *301 Ways to Have Fun at Work* (San Francisco: Berrett-Koehler, 1997).

31. Jackie Frieberg and Kevin Frieberg, *Nuts!* (Austin, Tex.: Bard, 1996), 247.

32. Susan Vaughn, "To Think Out of the Box, Get Back into the Sandbox," *Los Angeles Times*, 11 January 1999, Careers section, pp. 3, 13.

33. Jude T. Rich, "Sitting on a Gold Mine: Reducing Employee Turnover at All Costs," *World at Work* (2nd quarter 2002): 44.

34. Christina Melnarik, "Retaining High Tech Professionals: Constructive and Destructive Responses to Job Dissatisfaction among Electrical Engineers and Non-Engineering Professionals" (Ph.D. diss., Walden University, 1998).

35. Beverly Kaye and Beverly Bernstein, "Mentworking: Building Learning Relationships for the 21st Century," workshop materials, Career Systems International, Inc., Scranton, Pa., 1998, 45.

36. Ibid., 67.

37. Joan Fleischer Tamen, "Good Mentor Can Be a Guardian Angel in Business," *South Florida Sun-Sentinel*, 26 April 2004.

38. Beverly Kaye, adapted from "Career Development—Anytime, Anyplace," *Training & Development* 47 (December 1993): 46–50.

39. Daniel Goleman, *Working with Emotional Intelligence* (New York: Bantam, 1998).

40. Paul G. Stoltz, *Adversity Quotient* (New York: Wiley, 1997).

41. Adapted with permission from "Run the Numbers," Career Systems International, Scranton, Pa., 2000.

42. Rich, "Sitting on a Gold Mine."

43. Sharon Jordan-Evans and Beverly Kaye, "Opportunity Mine-ing," workshop materials, Career Systems International, Inc., Scranton, Pa., 1998.

44. Edward F. Murphy, *2,715 One-Line Quotations for Speakers, Writers, and Raconteurs* (New York: Crown, 1981), 148.

45. Ibid.

46. David Champion, "Mastering the Value Chain: An Interview with Mark Levin of Millennium Pharmaceuticals," *Harvard Business Review* (June 2001): 109–115.

47. Po Bronson, *What Should I Do with My Life?* (New York: Random House, 2002), 363.

48. Marilee Adams, *Change Your Questions, Change Your Life* (San Francisco: Berrett-Koehler, 2004), 47.

49. Gerald Ledford Jr. and Peter LeBlanc, *World at Work* 9, no. 3 (third quarter 2000): 1–11.

50. Ken Blanchard and Spencer Johnson, *The One Minute Manager* (New York: Morrow, 1982).

51. "Cash and Praise a Powerful Combo," *Incentive Magazine*, 1 June 2003.

52. John A. Byrne, "How to Lead Now: Getting Extraordinary Performance When You Can't Pay for It,"*FastCompany* (August 2003).

53. "Your Place or Mine?" *CFO Magazine – IT Edition* (March 2004).

54. Jennifer Oldman, "Remote Control," *Los Angeles Times*, 8 June 1998.

55. James C. Collins and Jerry I. Porras, *Built to Last* (New York: HarperBusiness, 1994), 119.

56. Gene J. Koprowski, "Flexibility in the Workplace Is an Increasing Concern," *Information Week* (10 October 2000): 212.

57. "More Employers Offer Work/Life Benefits to Gain Edge in Tight Labor Market," The Hewitt Work/Life Survey, company press release, 4 May 2000.

58. Megan Lisagor, "Flextime: Not a Bad Stretch," *Federal Computer Week*, 29 March 2004.

59. Donna Fenn, "Personnel Best," *Inc.* (February 2000): 75.

60. Rob Heneman, David Greenberger, Stephen Strasser, and Gayle Porter, "Link between Worker Pay and Satisfaction," *Journal of Business and Psychology* (2004).

61. Morgan W. McCall, Michael M. Lombardo, and A. Morrison, *The Lessons of Experience* (Lexington, Mass.: Lexington Books, 1988); and Morgan W. McCall, *High Flyers* (Cambridge, Mass.: Harvard Business School Press, 1998).

62. Published by Lominger, Minneapolis, Minn., 2001.

63. Susan H. Sorrells, "A Workplace without Turnover? Making It a Reality," *HR.com*, 18 March 2003.

64. Robert B. Catell and Kenny Moore, with Glenn Rifkin, *The CEO and the Monk: One Company's Journey to Profit and Purpose* (Hoboken, N.J.: Wiley, 2004), 235.

65. Katherine Thornberry, "Valley Firms Get Creative to Retain Hot Employees," *Business Journal of San Jose,* 1 June 1998.

66. "Invest in Your Values: A Self-Assessment Instrument," Career Systems International, Scranton, Pa., 1999.

67. Richard Leider and David Shapiro, *Whistle While You Work: Heeding Your Life's Calling* (San Francisco: Berrett-Koehler, 2001).

68. SHRM/USA Today.com Job Satisfaction Poll, 2002.

69. Laurent Belsie, "Weeks Worth," *Christian Science Monitor*, Work & Money section, 23 August 2004.

70. Michael J. Weiss, "Is Your Job Making You Sick?" *Better Homes & Garden* (September 2004).

71. Susan Mitchell, *American Generations: Who They Are, How They Live, What They Think* (Ithaca, N.Y.: New Strategist, 1998).

72. Adapted with permission from Devon Scheef and Diane Thielfoldt, The Learning Café, Thousand Oaks, Calif., 2000.

73. Ibid.

74. *Workforce Management* (February 2004): 43–48.

75. See www.bls.giv/emp.

76. Chuck Raasch, Gannett News Service, 25 March 2003.

77. Deborah Parkinson, "Voice of Experience: Mature Workers in the Future Workforce," November 2002, Conference Board, R-1319-02-RR.

78. Brad Foss, "Interest in Older Employees Rises as Seniors in Confront the Need to Work," *Miami Herlad*, 22 June 2004.

79. *Hartford Courant*, 21 June 2004.

80. Marshall Goldsmith, "Adding Value—But at What Cost?" *Fast Company* (August 2003).

81. See www.bls.gov/emp.

82. *Workforce Management*, 1 March 2004.

83. See www.gallupjournal.com/CA/ee/20020603.asp.

84. See http://money.cnn.com/2003/11/11/pf/q_iquit/index.htm?cnn=yes.

85. Saratoga Institute, "Study of the Emerging Workforce."

86. "Linking Employee Satisfaction with Productivity, Performance, and Customer Satisfaction," www.corporateleadershipcouncil.com.

Index

About the Authors

The authors of this book began their journey together when they collected the research for the first edition of *Love 'Em or Lose 'Em*, published in 1999. They were passionate about providing managers with practical tools and strategies for engaging, developing, and retaining the talent on their teams. They still are.

Bev (right) is a Jersey girl who (for the past 30 years) has made her home in Los Angeles with her husband Barry, teenage daughter Lindsey, and Roxy (part Dalmatian, part terrier). Bev has been involved in this work for close to 30 years and is CEO and founder of Career Systems International. She holds a doctorate from UCLA. Her first book, *Up Is Not the Only Way*, became a classic in the field. With the help of the CSI core staff and the consulting and training team, she has been able to deliver career development, mentoring, engagement, and retention initiatives on a global scale. She is a sought-after keynote speaker and a bit of an energizer bunny.

Sharon (left) was born and bred in the Northwest but now lives with her husband Mike and Oreo, a very smart Shih-Tzu, in Cambria, California (near the ocean and the woods). She has four grown children and three adorable grandchildren. She holds a master's degree in organizational development. After a number of leadership positions in the corporate and consulting world, she formed her own organization, the Jordan Evans Group. She spends her professional time in executive coaching, employee engagement consulting, and keynote speaking, where she has gained international prominence. She also serves as a resource for a number of national media. Sharon does a great job of balancing work and life and is a role model for Bev in that regard.

Working with the Authors

Sharon and Bev speak internationally on engagement and retention-related topics. Recent keynote speeches include:

- *Engaging the Heart and the Mind: Top 10 How-Tos*
- *Winning the War for Talent: Are You in Shape?*
- *Both Sides Now: Manager and Employee Roles in Workplace Satisfaction*
- *High-Performing Leaders Give Attention to Retention*
- *Employee Development: A Critical Engagement Factor*

In addition, Bev and Sharon provide specialized services to organizations and individuals. You can learn more about them by visiting their joint site, www.keepem.com, or by linking to their company sites, below.

Career Systems International—A Beverly Kaye Company

Career Systems International transforms organizational talent initiatives into results-driven actions by delivering flexible, engaging, and practical solutions designed to encourage, enlighten, and equip today's workforce. Bev has devoted over 25 years to developing and delivering award-winning workshops, solutions, assessments, and services to international clients that increase workforce engagement, productivity, and profitability. With a broad emphasis on retaining, engaging, and developing key talent, Career Systems' programs build effective partnerships between employees and their managers using a variety of modalities, including facilitator-led workshops and on-line, self-paced, or blended learning experiences.

Career Systems International
2300 Stafford Avenue, Suite 500
Scranton, Pennsylvania 18505
Phone: 800-577-6916
Fax: 570-346-8606
Web site: www.CareerSystemsIntl.com
E-mail: HQ@csibka.com

Sharon Jordan-Evans and the Jordan Evans Group

Sharon Jordan-Evans is president of the Jordan Evans Group, a leadership consulting firm. Prior to starting her own business in 1996, Sharon served as senior vice president and consulting partner for one of the world's leading transition management consulting firms. She specializes in executive coaching and works with both high-potentials and senior-level leaders. Sharon also speaks and consults internationally on the topic of employee engagement and retention, working with organizations from such diverse industries as health care, high technology, financial services, entertainment, computers, and insurance. Her international experience includes work in Switzerland, Australia, the U.K., Canada, and Mexico.

Jordan Evans Group
565 Chiswick Way
Cambria, California 93428
Phone: 805-927-1432
Fax: 805-927-7756
Web site: www.jeg.org
E-mail: sharon@jeg.org

A *Learning Event* for Managers
Building Loyalty and Commitment in Your Workplace

We know that managers can greatly influence employee levels of engagement and increase their likelihood of staying. But often these leaders need tools and tune-ups.

Love 'Em or Lose 'Em: Building Loyalty and Commitment in the Workplace is a flexible and engaging manager's workshop developed by the authors. The workshop uses self-assessment tools, action-based activities and practice exercises to help managers integrate the concepts of *Love 'Em or Lose 'Em* into everyday work life. It can be delivered as a facilitated workshop experience, on-line self-study, or blended offering. It's organized around these seven messages:

- **Talent in the Spotlight**—Key concepts and facts supporting the criticality of talent management

- **People Stay for More Than Pay**—Personal motivators, retention drivers, and other talent insights

- **The Buck Stops Here**—Reinforces the power and influence of the manager

- **Am I a Talent Magnet?**—Assesses strengths and opportunities for improvement as a talent-focused manager

- **Ask So You Don't Have to Guess**—Planning and skill-building process

- **Strategies That Work**—26 strategies to improve retention and engagement

- **From Ask to Action, Making It Happen**—Designing and prioritizing action-based retention and engagement plans

Managers will walk away with the ownership of the role, skills to succeed, actions to implement, and a process to follow.

To experience the **on-line offering** of this program and tools, visit http://leleonline.com/lele_demo/. For more information call Career Systems International, 800-577-6916, e-mail HQ@csibka.com or visit www.KeepEm.com.

Ongoing Research
Want THE LATEST FINDINGS?

The authors and their organizations have been conducting engagement and retention surveys for the past several years. The following surveys, along with instant findings, are available to help support your engagement and retention efforts. They can be accessed at http://www.keepem.com/ResearchSurveys.asp

☆ ☆ ☆ ☆ ☆ ☆ ☆ ☆ ☆ ☆ ☆ ☆ ☆ ☆ ☆

What Kept You?

An ongoing research study conducted by Career Systems International

We've asked more than 16,000 people to date the question "What Kept You?" at the job they really loved. The constantly updated survey findings help you prioritize potential engagement and retention strategies by identifying the top ten engagement and retention drivers by age, industry, gender, job level, company size, job function and geography.

☆ ☆ ☆ ☆ ☆ ☆ ☆ ☆ ☆ ☆ ☆ ☆ ☆ ☆ ☆

What Would Make You Walk?

Thousands continue to answer the question "what would drive you right out the door?" in this survey of highly detrimental jerk behaviors. Take the survey and then immediately find out not only the rank-ordered jerk behaviors that would cause employees to leave, but also the behaviors you as an engaging team leader need to avoid.

SatisfACTION Requires ACTION

What Matters Most in Workforce Satisfaction?

Through this survey thousands of people have selected five actions they believe they should take, out of 26 possible work "satis*factors*". The real-time ranked findings are presented by age, gender, job level, industry, company size, job function and geography. Take the survey and in the process learn about the actions identified by your peers and others as key to their workplace satisfaction.

So *You* Love 'Em . . . But *Do They Love It?*

Berrett-Koehler Publishers

"My boss was reading Love 'Em or Lose 'Em and remarked how he already knows most of this, but isn't doing it. I told him the authors are coming out with a companion guide for employees—one that gives them strategies and ideas for getting more of what they want right where they are (instead of quickly jumping ship). He said to me, 'You have my permission to buy a copy for everyone of our employees the minute this book comes out!' I couldn't believe it. He's never done that before."

—Nursing Supervisor, large healthcare organization

After **Love 'Em or Lose 'Em** was completed, the authors said, "Now it's the employees' turn." So **Love It, Don't Leave It: 26 Ways to Get What You Want at Work** was born and quickly reached the WSJ best-seller list.

In this book, Bev and Sharon draw on years of experience as management and career consultants to present twenty-six innovative strategies for enhancing one's current work situation. Chock full of quizzes, self-interviews, case studies, anecdotes, and tips, **Love It, Don't Leave It** covers a myriad of workplace issues—from making the job more interesting and reducing stress to adding a sense of fun to the workplace; from bridging the generation gap with coworkers to finding passion for one's work.

The first step to improving any work situation is to speak up. "If you don't ask, you're less likely to get what you want," they explain. Most employees don't talk to their managers when they are unhappy. They expect bosses to know that something is wrong without being told. **Love It, Don't Leave It** includes a three-step process for speaking up effectively:

- **Get Crystal Clear About What You Want**—The authors include a self-interview to help readers figure out what they really want at work.

- **Consider Who, When and How You'll Ask**—The authors explain how to pick the best person, time, and way to ask for a change. *(continued)*

■ **Identify the Barriers, Then Bulldoze Them**—The authors show how to overcome one's own fears as well as the boss' mindset, constraints, and concerns to get what is truly desired. And if the answer is still no, *Love It, Don't Leave It* provides hints for continuing the dialogue until success is achieved.

The second principle for creating a great job is taking responsibility for one's own situation. "Don't pass the buck," the authors insist. "Some people are tempted to hold others accountable for their work satisfaction. Most find over time that those others can't, or won't, deliver what's wanted and needed."

Finally, *Love It, Don't Leave It* provides suggested steps for taking control of one's work life, setting career goals, developing new skills, finding a mentor, and taking advantage of new opportunities. "You own your career. Take steps now to plan it, build it, and strengthen it," write Kaye and Jordan-Evans.

Following this advice is one of many steps to carving out the perfect job. And this is just the tip of the iceberg. According to Kaye and Jordan-Evans, anyone can create the job they love. It is up to the individual. "Yes, there are actions your manager can take, and yes, there are actions your organizational leaders can take, but in the end it's all up to you." *Love It, Don't Leave It* will help every employee become engaged and involved in developing a more satisfactory, creative, and exciting workplace. Its key message is:

Make the job you have the job you LOVE.

Paperback original, 225 pages, ISBN 1-57675-250-X
Visit **www.loveitdontleaveit.com** to order and download the first three chapters.